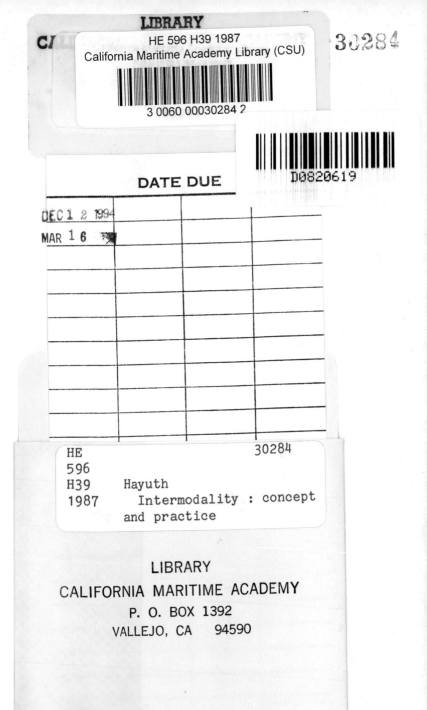

INTERMODALITY:
CONCEPT AND PRACTICE

STRUCTURAL CHANGES IN THE
OCEAN FREIGHT TRANSPORT INDUSTRY

by

Yehuda Hayuth, Ph.D.

*Israel Shipping and Aviation
Research Institute*

|L|L|P|

LONDON   NEW YORK   HAMBURG   HONG KONG
LLOYD'S OF LONDON PRESS LTD
1987

Lloyd's of London Press Ltd.
Sheepen Place, Colchester, Essex, CO3 3LP
Great Britain

USA AND CANADA
Lloyd's of London Press Inc.
Suite 523, 611 Broadway
New York, NY 10012 USA

GERMANY
Lloyd's of London Press
PO Box 11 23 47, Deichstrasse 41
2000 Hamburg 11
West Germany

SOUTH-EAST ASIA
Lloyd's of London Press (Far East) Ltd.
903 Chung Nam Building
1 Lockhart Road, Wanchai
Hong Kong
©
Yehuda Hayuth

First published 1987

British Library Cataloguing in Publication Data
Hayuth, Yehuda
Intermodality : concept and practice.
1. Cargo handling —— Law and legislation
2. Ships —— Cargo —— Law and legislation
I. Title
341.7'5668 K1176

ISBN 1-85044-146-4

Text typeset in 11pt on 12pt Goudy Old Style by
TND Serif Ltd., Hadleigh, Suffolk
Printed in Great Britain by WBC Print Ltd., Bristol

To
Ruth, Shiri and Ori
with admiration

Acknowledgments

I wish to express my thanks and appreciation to Prof. N. Wydra, Director of the Israel Shipping and Aviation Research Institute and a former General Manager of Zim Shipping Co., on whose knowledge and vast experience I could always rely.

Thanks also are extended to A. M. Goldstein, for his helpful editorial assistance, and to Mrs I Kolar and Mrs G. Breitstein, for their typing of the manuscript. The illustrations were prepared by the Cartographic Laboratory at the London School of Economics and by Miss A. Gold at the University of Haifa.

Y.H.

Table of contents

List of tables

List of figures

CHAPTER 1

Introduction

Over a span of thousands of years, the introduction of the sail, invention of the compass, development of the steamship, introduction of iron hulls, and, in a much different vein, the recognition of the freedom of the seas have all been milestones for the shipping industry. Each of these breakthroughs had its impact on trade routes and on the rise and decline of shipping lines and ports. Until the last century and a half, however, the rate of change was rather slow. There was not much difference between the structure of the ancient vessels that sailed the Mediterranean 3,000 years ago and that of the ships of the eighteenth century. There had been virtually no advances in the methods of cargo handling, which entailed either manual or crude mechanical loading of materials in bulk or, sometimes, in packaged, baled or crated units. During the last few decades, however, ocean transportation has experienced rapid changes. Not only have the size and draft of ships increased spectacularly, rendering many older ports unusable and many conventional ships obsolete, but the methods of handling cargo have been drastically modified. Containerization and the development of intermodal transport systems have had a profound effect on the shipping industry, its structure, operation, and management.

The movement of goods in a single container by more than one mode of transportation was an important development in the transport industry and for all the elements involved in international and domestic trade. Indeed, containerization and, more recently, multi-modality — or as it is commonly called, intermodality — have caused a tremendous impact on every facet of the transport industry. Who would have predicted that the experimental journey of the *Ideal X* from the Port of New York on April 26, 1956, and the inaugural sailing from San Francisco on August 31, 1958, of Matson's *Hawaiian Merchant*, a converted C-3 freighter, were to pioneer a new transport concept, one that would revolutionize the entire transportation industry a decade later? Who would have dared forecast just a decade ago the future impact of intermodality on the organization, operations, and structure of transportation and international trade?

Containerization has become the dominant method of transporting break of bulk goods in international trade. This is certainly true in the ocean-borne trade among developed countries, and the system is gradually spreading to the developing world, as well. Although containerization can be viewed as one of the latest developments in the transport industry, it is also possible to state that by the beginning of the 1980s containerization in its conventional form was already a mature system. The maximum containership size in 1980 was basically the same as it was a decade earlier. Ship-to-shore operations were being performed by essentially the same gantry cranes for nearly two decades, although some modifications had been introduced over the years. The trend of constant improvement in shipping and port productivity characterizing so much of the early stages of containerization was moderated.

Containerization, nevertheless, is still viewed largely in terms of a revolutionary technological change in cargo handling. Indeed, during the first two decades of this transport method, the main efforts and investments of the transport modes involved were devoted to the construction of new cellular container vessels, newly designed container terminals, and specialized container handling cranes. Since the early 1980s, however, the transportation system has been undergoing a new phase of change, characterized not so much by technological innovation as by the alteration of the organizational, logistical, and regulatory structure of the transport industry. Furthermore, the principal components of the container system — the shipping lines, ports, and railways — are even now undergoing fundamental change. In this conceptual metamorphosis of the cargo transport system, container movements are increasingly being viewed in the light of the total, integrated distribution system. Containerization is now the common denominator of a growing *intermodal* transport system.

Yet another development in the international trade arena has greatly affected the transportation system. The structural changes in the world's economy, such as the rapid diffusion of multinational corporations, the process of the industrialization of developing countries and the de-industrialization of developed countries, and the emergence of the Pacific Ocean as a major trade centre, somewhat at the expense of the traditional major trade zone, the Atlantic, have all brought about and promoted the globalization of the world economy. The scale of operation of the industrial entrepreneur, the trading house, and the transportation company has been greatly expanded geographically. The shipping industry, for one, has been gradually adapting itself to these developments. The process bears with it a fundamental challenge to the foundations of the traditional shipping industry; the basic structure of the shipping company, the functions under its responsibility, the spatial scale of its operation, the competitive environment of the industry, and even the liner conference system have all been challenged.

On the North American scene, there is a relaxation of the once strictly regulated environment that characterized the transport industry of the United States. The deregulation of the trucking industry and of the railways in 1980 and the US Shipping Act of 1984 had the effect of advancing the development of the intermodal movements of containerized cargo. In doing so, these measures effectively have enhanced a closer cooperation and integration of the various transport modes and elevated the practice of containerization and the intermodal transport concept to an entirely new level.

The objective of this book is to evaluate the changes in direction and emphasis that have taken place — and are still taking place — in the international and domestic freight transportation system and to analyse their impact on maritime transportation and its related industries. It is the aim of this book to raise the measure of awareness of the participating parties, at all levels, in the international trade arena to: (a) the ever-changing nature of the industry in which they are operating; (b) the dynamic characteristics of the functions of each of the principal components of the transport system — ocean transportation, sea ports, inland transportation, and physical distribution; and (c) the changing scale of operation, both functionally and geographically, of the individual transport modes and of the integrated transport system. It is hoped that in an era of wide-ranging permutations in international trade and the freight transport industry, an analysis of general trends in the transportation of ocean-borne trade and in related transport modes, and the formulation of several conceptual frameworks, will impart a more comprehensive understanding of the key issues and problems involved, and thus contribute to a better, more efficient transport system.

Moderation in the rate of technological change and innovation began to characterize the ocean transport system in the mid-1980s. On the other hand, the advent of the intermodal transport system established a second phase in the containerization era. The definition, general implications, and conceptual component of intermodal transport are discussed in Chapter 2, followed by an analysis, in Chapter 3, of selected intermodal transport sub-systems. The following three chapters analyse the impact of the new transport concept on the structure and characteristics of the relevant transport modes. The main theme of Chapter 4 is the structural change and the rationalization that the shipping industry is going through in the process of adapting itself to intermodality. Chapter 5 focuses on the changing role of seaports in the total transport chain, while Chapter 6 directs its discussion to the inland segments of freight transportation. Chapter 7 analyses the growing importance of logistics and the physical distribution concept in the total transport system, and the penultimate chapter (Chapter 8) devotes its discussion to the changing nature of competition and complementarity among all the transport modes. The final chapter (Chapter 9) offers several conclusions about the present state and future prospects of intermodality.

CHAPTER 2

The concept of intermodal transport

THE TRANSPORTATION SYSTEM — CONCEPTUAL ANALYSIS

Transportation may be viewed as a technological and organizational system that aims to transfer people and goods from one place to another in order to balance the spatial and economic gap between demand and supply centres. That gap might be on a local, regional, national, continental, or even global scale. The *total* transport concept approaches transportation from a comprehensive and inclusive viewpoint, while carefully analysing the role of each component of the system in light of the interrelations of all the variables of which the system is composed. The total transportation concept also recognizes that transportation itself does not operate in a vacuum; it is a subsystem of a much wider and complex economic, political, and social structure.

Transportation, like many other systems in our society, has been changing rapidly over the last several decades. Any attempt to evaluate and analyse these changes must first consider the principal components of the system and the available options. Options, or decision variables, are those aspects of transportation that can be changed directly by the decisions of individuals, groups, or institutions.[1] In the case of international trade, the options available can be divided into two groups: those dealing with the transportation system itself; and those dealing with the political, economic, and social environments that provide the framework within which the transportation system operates.

1. Manheim, M. L. (1974), *Fundamentals of Transportation System Analysis* (Cambridge: MIT, Preliminary Edition).

A. THE SYSTEM OPTIONS

The "decision variables" or options for transportation may be divided into five major groups. Although each group has been considered separately, it is the basic rationale of the system concept that all variables are closely related. The options are as follows: technology, networks, transport modes, information and communications, and logistics. These variables are all exposed to a wide spectrum of decisions and options that can be exercised with regard to each one of them separately or in one or more combinations. All are greatly influenced by a variety of elements directly or indirectly involved in the transportation industry and international trade. The five variables are represented through four major viewpoints: that of the user, the operator, the socio-politico-economic system, and the government (see Figure 1).

1. Technology

Decision-making as well as analysis of either conventional or changing technology in transportation may be divided into three principal dimensions.[2] The first is mode and equipment design. The last three decades have witnessed the development of new types of vessels in the international trade arena: cellular container vessels, roll-on/roll-off ships, LASH, conbulk vessels, among others. Similarly new designs of cargo-handling units have appeared: containers, gantry cranes, even the slurry system — all of them representing new technology. The second dimension is the means of propulsion, whether the economically designed marine diesel engines that have come on stream in the 1980s and the newly designed sails that are being tested even now; or the jet engine in civilian air transportation and the new propfan engine currently being developed by aircraft manufacturers. The third dimension of technological options in transportation is vehicle size: very large crude carrier (VLCC), ultra-large crude carrier (ULCC), Panamax-size container vessel, and the wide body jet airplane; also, the variety of shapes of transferable units (e.g., 40, 45 or 48-foot containers).

---

2. On technological progress in shipping see: Abrahamsson, B. J. (1980), *International Ocean Shipping: Current Concepts and Principles* (Boulder: Westview Press), pp. 57–60.

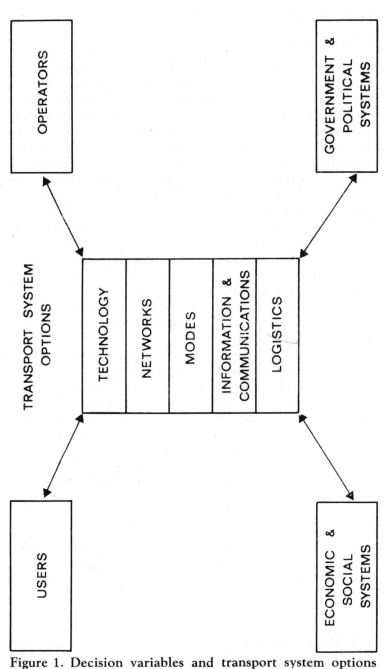

Figure 1. Decision variables and transport system options

2. Networks

Transport networks may be defined by a set of links and nodes. Links correspond to transport routes, such as rail lines, shipping routes, airways, highways, or navigable rivers. The nodes represent the intersection points of the network and express the connectivity relations of the links in the system. Seaports, airports, and rail terminals are a few common examples of nodes. The conventional function of nodes in the transport network was to transfer goods or people from one mode of transportation to another. The term "break of bulk" points, which had commonly been used in the transportation literature, and the term "terminal" indicate more than anything else the end of the involvement of one transport mode and the beginning of the service of another mode. These conventional functions of the nodes began gradually to change in the 1970s, with more emphasis being placed on connectivity and continuation than "terminus". The transportation nodes are now perceived more as a link in the transport chain — a link that must be overcome quickly and efficiently — rather than as a final stop for a transport mode.

Networks represent the supply side of the transportation system. They provide the infrastructure for the various modes and allow the basic conditions for the flow of the cargo. The quality of each transport network in current terms is determined by the characteristics of each of the components of the network; that is, the degree of connectivity between the links or the relative contribution of a single element to the total system. The quality of a network is greatly affected, as might be expected, by the weakest link in the transport chain. A shallow-draft port in a specific region, for example, may affect the entire transportation system, much beyond the issue of measured productivity at the specific port.

Transportation networks must always be analysed in conjunction with other elements of the transportation system, such as modes, commodity-flow characteristics, and institutional frameworks.

3. Transport modes

The transportation modes are the means by which cargo is

transferred from one place to another. There are five prominent modes of transport: motor-vehicle land transport, rail transport, water transportation, air transport, and pipelines. The conventional analysis of transport modes treats every mode individually. Indeed, each mode has its own economic structure and rationale; and although competition always existed among the various transport modes, it was particularly fierce within the modes themselves.

If the single mode was the basic element for consideration, it is wrong to perceive it as a unified one. A considerable variety of services and equipment exists within each mode: from the conventional general cargo ship to specialized bulk carriers, cellular container vessels, or barges in water transportation; from the conventional box car to the specialized twin-deck container cars in rail transportation; and so on. A great deal of development, both in technology and in organizational terms, has occurred at an accelerated rate since 1960 within each mode of transportation. Specialization is perhaps the most common phenomenon that characterizes the more recent developments.

Cooperation between various transport modes is not a new phenomenon. Rail-steamship cooperation existed in Europe and the United States in the late nineteenth century. Rail-truck cooperation has grown since the late 1960s, following the advent of containerization and the operation of various LCL services and "piggyback" trains. In air transportation, the introduction of a wide-body jet freighter in the mid-1970s promoted some measure of cooperation with other modes. Most of the modal-split freight analysis undertaken in transportation research refers mainly to the share of each mode in the total trade of a specific route; rarely is there an attempt to evaluate the degree of cooperation between or among the various modes.

The basic single-mode approach determined the transport industry up until one or two decades ago. This approach was paralleled by the structure of government offices and regulatory agencies dealing with transportation, particularly in the United States. The dominance of the single-mode approach has started to erode as the intermodal concept has begun to permeate the transport industry at an ever-growing pace. Despite the variety of problems that have accompanied the introduction of intermodal transportation, it is already legitimate to raise the question: does a single mode in the international trade arena today have the right to exist independently in a conventional manner? Although this question may not have a clear-cut answer, for there will always be various viewpoints, no one in the transport industry can ignore the question. This by itself hints at a possible revolution in the area of transportation-mode analysis.

4. Information and communications

Information systems and communication means and networks have been designed to achieve and maintain administrative and managerial control. Both types of control were always significant in the transportation industry; however, their role and importance have been tremendously intensified in temporal and spatial terms. In an era in which close cooperation and coordination within and between transport modes are among the most essential characteristics for the functional and economic survival of an integrated transport system, keeping track of hundreds and thousands of moving containers is a basic condition for their efficient utilization on all routes, encompassing all directions. With the potential tributary and marketing areas available to each mode having been vastly extended geographically, the command of fast, reliable information and communications is a primary condition for entering, let alone surviving, the harsh and complex integrated transport system.

5. Logistics

Transportation has for years been recognized, among its other roles, as a sub-function of logistics. The inter-relationship between logistics and transportation has now been so greatly strengthened that many even regard logistics as being synonymous with physical distribution, both involving pre-production and post-production control of material flows.[3] Today it is obvious that neither shippers nor transport operators can consider transportation and logistics individually. The decision-making process in one of these disciplines exerts a great effect on the other. It seems that the selection of routes and transport modes and decisions about the

3. Wallace, I. L. (1974), *Transportation Regulation, Management and National Policies* (Seattle: University of Washington Continuing Education).

location of an inland container depot or a specific marketing strategy are all part of the same system.

B. THE SYSTEM COMPONENTS

The *operator's viewpoint* represents a wide spectrum of decisions about how a transportation system should operate with maximum efficiency. Decisions may include not only route selection, modal choice, scheduling, and type of service offered, but even physical distribution and logistics. Particular emphasis is placed on the options involved in the structure of cargo flows. The organization of the flow of commodities is greatly affected by the spatial structure of demand and supply on various scales. The delivery of cargoes from production sites to consumption points requires a massive flow over a complex network system of links varying in length and capacity and employing multiple modes at different hierarchical orders. Moreover, it is only with the continuous movements of goods that the functional entities of each link or mode in the transport system can maintain a recognizable level of specialization. In order to achieve greater efficiency and to reduce the aggregate costs of the total transport system, a high level of managerial control and a rigid structuring of the cargo flow are needed. A high degree of coordination among all transportation elements is also absolutely vital for the maintenance and success of the system.

Currently, the main operators in the intermodal system are the conventional transport modes. In a transport system in which control of the cargo is turning out to be the key element, the involvement of a proliferation of new organizations in intermodal movements can be observed. Third-party non-equity participants like the non-vessel operating common carriers (NVOCCs), in particular, are taking an increasing share of the through-transport services. This growing involvement of NVOCCs in the market, furthermore, has broken up the traditional liner shipping market, in which the ship operator used to sell cargo space directly; now, the space-selling function is shared with entities that are not liner operators as such.

The *users*, the second viewpoint, traditionally had a considerable impact on the route and on the mode of transport that would carry their goods. The shipper is gradually losing influence on these decisions, now that a single carrier may control the entire voyage, using various transport modes through a multiple choice of alternative routes. Nevertheless, the user's impact on the transportation system has not entirely waned. The shippers are the ones responsible for creating demand levels in the transportation industry even if the spatial distribution of the producers and the consumers dictates the origin and destination points along the transport network. It was the level of demand for oil, for example, that brought about the construction of VLCCs. Similarly, the shippers' demand for general cargo carriers, imposed on the transport network of the 1950s and 1960s, was largely responsible for the introduction of containerization. Obviously, the selection of transport options regarding the technology, the modes, and the transport networks available has, in turn, a great impact on the users themselves.

The third component, the *social* and *economic systems*, is generally exogenous, although closely related to the transportation industry. These systems provide the basic framework in which the transportation system operates. They actually determine the level of demand for transportation services and, in turn, the spatial pattern and organizational structure of the transport operators. Although the various transport elements have very little impact on social and economic parameters, like the rate of economic growth or the level of inflation, any shift or change in production or consumption level — whether on a local or even a global scale — has an immediate effect on the transport modes or the structure of the transport network. On the other hand, the availability of efficient transport systems in a region may serve as a catalyst for social and economic growth.

It is obvious that a relaxation of the restrictions on capital flow, an expansion of multinational corporative activities, and a trend towards a globalization of the economy must invite an appropriate response by the transportation system.

The fourth and last viewpoint is that of *government* and the *political system*. Their impact on transportation differs from one country to another, depending on national policy and the level of government agency. At the local or municipal level, the primary concern is the direct impact of transportation on the inhabitants and the emphasis is on ensuring their well-being. At the state, regional, or federal level, the considerations are more general: economic, social, and political. Policies in these spheres dictate the level and form of government intervention in the transport industry. The power of government to impose regulations on such basic elements of transportation as the rate structure, mergers between transport modes, allocation of routes, and restrictions on vehicle dimensions is critical in its impact on the development of the shape and level of service of the transport industry. The decision of government to deregulate may have even greater significance. Deregulation, for instance, may enhance new investment in transportation; it may motivate entrepreneurs to introduce new technology in order to increase the efficiency of a mode. The relationship between transportation and government, however, is basically a two-way link. Thus, a choice of certain options by operators of the various elements of the transportation system may attract the attention of governmental agencies and invite them to intervene in the system.

THE INTERMODAL CONCEPT

The transportation industry and international trade have undergone vast changes since World War II. Three principal dimensions are responsible for and characterize the changes: demand for transportation; transport technology; and organization of the transportation system.

The improved economy of the Western World in the 1950s and 1960s and the stirring of some developing countries, particularly in South East Asia, in the 1970s exerted a direct impact on international trade. The volumes of cargo that, as a consquence, began moving internationally disrupted the equilibrium between demand for transportation and supply of transport units and facilities.

As the Western World recovered in the 1950s and early 1960s from the ravages of World War II, it generated general cargo trade, only to have the increased volumes come up against an older and older fleet of conventional general cargo vessels, inefficient port facilities, and cargo-handling methods not much different from those employed earlier in the century. Slow turn around of ships and heavy congestion in ports were an unavoidable result of the inability of the transport system to meet the demands of international trade. A drastic change was clearly needed, and it came in the form of technological innovation: in cargo-handling methods, in ship design, and in port facilities. Unitization, containerization, cellular ships, roll-on/roll-off vessels, and gantry cranes comprise but some of this innovation characterizing the technology and leading to the changes that took place during the 1960s and 1970s.

The major technological innovations, though, had essentially come about in the late 1950s and early 1960s. By the 1980s, two decades had passed with no further revolutionary changes in containership design or size or in cargo-handling techniques and with almost the same gantry cranes and container terminal operation methods. The scene was set and ready, perhaps past due, for a new phase of transport development. Intermodality, the new development, also brought with it a shift in emphasis compared to containerization. Instead of hardware, the focus was on the organization of the transport industry and the synchronization of the distribution system. The following table clearly illustrates this change — the technological nature of most of the key elements in the containerization concept compared to the organizational features informing the principal components of the newly developed intermodal transport system.

Ten key elements in containerization and intermodality

Containerization	Intermodality
1. Unitization	1. System concept
2. Standardization	2. Management and coordination
3. Cellular ships	3. Control over cargo
4. Roll-on/roll-off vessels	4. Mergers
5. Gantry Cranes	5. Multi-modal companies
6. Straddle carriers	6. Modal integration
7. Specialized terminals	7. Through rates and billing
8. Ship-to-shore productivity	8. Information system
9. Terminal back-up land	9. Physical distribution
10. Multi-rate structure	10. Deregulation

In the conceptual metamorphosis of the transportation system, cargo movements are viewed in the light of the total distribution system. Included in such a total system are producers, shippers, ocean and land carriers, ports, inventory control, warehousing, and freight forwarding organizations. Such a system implies close cooperation and coordination among these elements. The physical distribution of cargo, then, involves an integrated logistical system, in which the justification for a single mode of transportation to exist as an independent operator has been weakening. Thus, the relevance and effectiveness of seagoing vessels, trucks, railroads, and ports are evaluated in relation to their roles as individual elements within a total system. Almost any new development, investment, or decision made by ocean and land carriers today takes full account of the whole picture of an integrated transportation-distribution system.

Intermodality, thus, is simply defined as the movement of cargo from shipper to consignee by at least two different modes of transport under a single rate, through-billing, and through-liability. The objective of intermodal transportation is to transfer goods in an continuous flow through the entire transport chain, from origin to final destination, in the most cost- and time-effective way. This means capitalizing on the relative advantages of various transport modes in every segment of the journey. An important part of the intermodal concept is the carrier's ability to provide the shipper with a single rate, reflected in a through-billing, for the entire journey. That structure contrasts with the complicated multi-rate structure that usually prevailed (Figure 2).

In order to achieve this objective of intermodality, intensive cooperation and coordination among transportation modes are essential. It is, in fact, the degree of cooperation and the extent of the mutual commitments among the various elements of the transport system that mark the intermodal concept. Carriers can no longer operate on the basis of maximizing their own profits and displaying no regard for other links in the transportation – distribution system. A transport mode may not, as it once did, consider itself as a seller of a single, and a separate, route service within a marketing arena. As a result, all the relevant transport modes, without exception, are adapting themselves, or being adapted to, the requirements of the intermodal era. One of the most significant phenomena that has characterized containerized trade in the 1980s is the increased coordination and integration displayed by shipping lines, ports, and railways. There are, in fact, signs indicating that intermodality might bring about the establishment of large, multi-modal transport companies.

At the international level, attempts to confront the issue of

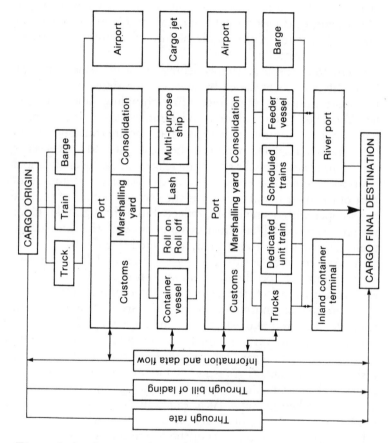

Figure 2. A schematic through flow of cargo from origin to final destination

intermodal transport are not new. As early as 1911, during discussions of the proposed "International Code of Affreightment",[4] efforts were made to set up an adequate legal framework for multimodal transport operations. During this period, however, transportation was above all a segmented industry based on unimodal operations and contracts. Any practice of multimodal transportation on the international scene was certainly marginal; in fact, a similar scale of operation for the concept prevailed through the 1960s. Only with containerization, particularly since the late 1970s, did multimodal services gain momentum.

On May 24, 1980, the final act of the "United Nations Conference on a Convention on International Multimodal Transport of Goods" was signed in Geneva under the auspices of UNCTAD, following resolution 33/160, adopted by the United Nations General Assembly on December 20, 1978.[5] The convention was signed by a wide spectrum of countries, from the developed to the developing countries, which recognized the following:

(a) that international multimodal transport is one means of facilitating the orderly expansion of world trade;

(b) the need to stimulate the development of smooth, economic, and efficient multimodal transport services adequate for the requirements of the trade concerned;

(c) the desirability of ensuring the orderly development of international multimodal transport in the interest of all countries and the need to consider the special problems of transit countries;

(d) the desirability of determining certain rules relating to the carriage of goods by international multimodal transport contracts, including equitable provisions concerning the liability of multimodal transport operators;

(e) that the convention did not affect the application of any international convention or national law relating to the regulation and control of transport operations;

4. Faust, P. (1985), "Multimodal Transport" in *Port Management Textbook — Containerization* (Bremen: Institute of Shipping Economics and Logistics), p. 227.

5. The UN Convention on International Multimodal Transport of Goods consists of seven parts: general provisions, documentation, liability of multimodal operator, liability of the consignor, claims and actions, supplementary provisions, and final clauses.

(f) the right of each state to regulate and control, at the national level, multimodal transport operators and operations;

(g) the need to have regard for the special interests and problems of developing countries — for example, the introduction of new technologies, participation in multimodal services by their national carriers and operators, cost efficiency, and maximum use of local labour and insurance;

(h) the need to ensure a balance of interests between suppliers and users of multimodal transport services; and

(i) the need to facilitate customs procedures, giving due consideration to the problem of transit countries.[6]

International multimodal transport was defined in the convention as the carriage of goods by at least two different modes of transport on the basis of a multimodal transport contract from a place in one country at which the goods are taken in charge by a multimodal operator to a place designated for delivery that is situated in a different country. The convention is based on an agreement that the shippers' freedom to choose between a multimodal or unimodal transport service must be maintained; and that multimodal transport operators, shippers, and their organizations and national authorities should be consulted before and after any introduction of new technology related to this transport concept. Although the convention provides a framework for the organization of multimodal transportation on the international level, only a few countries — far fewer than the required 30 countries for the act to enter into force — have so far become contracting parties. Nevertheless, intermodal activities in many countries, particularly in the Western world, are already substantial.

Indeed, the very pace of advancement of intermodal transportation has justified defining the concept as a new phase of transport development. Despite the hesitations and criticism, which resemble the initial reluctance to enter the containerization era, the level of current commitments to intermodality by the leading companies in the industry implies that a transport carrier,

6. United Nations Conference on Trade and Development (1981), *United Nations Conference on a Convention on International Multimodal Transport*, Final Act (New York: United Nations), p. 5.

either sea-going, land-based, or even airborne, cannot afford to stand idle and passively watch developments.

Intermodality in its purest form has tremendous potential for the transportation industry at large. In its ideal form, intermodality represents a case in which the total system exceeds the value of the sum of its individual transportation segments. Nevertheless, many problems, questions, and even doubts still remain with regard to the vitality and success of the concept. The issues relate to profitability, equipment, standardization, level of cooperation among transport modes, variety of approaches to the actual practices of intermodal transport, and the feasibility of the diffusion of the concept on a global scale.

The argument has been advanced, even by participants, that the resource capital and efforts required to expand the volume of intermodal traffic may not yield the appropriate return. Another reservation that has been voiced is that intermodal transportation, after its initial stages, has not produced the revenues anticipated and that the profit margin — if at all — is very thin. Shipping companies lay the blame on the severe competition between sea-going carriers and the consequent low level of freight rates. Seaports raise the issue of over-capacity. Most of the transport elements, but particularly the railroads, point to labour costs and the constant demand for new equipment as burdening their attempts to make intermodal transportation profitable. At the organizational level, the fact that, so far, there is no commonly accepted documentation among the transport operators, customs houses, and financial institutions to facilitate the through movement of cargo has been a major drawback, as the issue of the liability of the multimodal transport operator has yet to be settled.[7]

In its initial stage, intermodality required relatively small modifications in equipment. Containers on freight cars (COFC) and trailers on flat cars (TOFC) were transported on conventional rail cars. The growth in the volume of intermodal traffic, however, particularly in the United States, led to demands for new

7. Some progress has been made toward a standard form of multimodal document with the proposed UN-Multidoc. See: UNCTAD, *Multimodal Transport and Containerization*. Elaboration of a standard form and model provisions for multimodal transport documents, 10 September 1986 (GE 86-56994).

equipment and a wide range of facilities, from new intermodal freight stations and the relocation of railheads closer to or within the ports to double-stack container cars and Road Railer cars.

Standardization, associated with containerization, is yet another issue that has lately come to the fore. Some shipping lines, acting from their own considerations, have introduced non-ISO-size containers. Some container lines, for example, use 45-foot containers and want to employ even larger units. Truckers, for their part, have shown interest in increasing the length and height of containers, which they believe will improve truck utilization. This trend, however, is not accepted throughout the world, and variations occur even within continents. The rapid expansion of domestic intermodality in the United States led to the operation of two separate and non-compatible intermodal systems: the international system, restricted by vessel configuration to 20 and 40-foot steamship containers; and the domestic system, primarily based on 45 and 48-foot equipment.

On the surface, the impression is given that because transport modes seem to be cooperating more than ever and coordinating some of their moves, all is in harmony; in reality, much antagonism and lack of trust still exist between modes. This situation is partly due to a lack of knowledge, with the management and personnel of the individual transport modes insufficiently informed of one another's economics and rationale. Indeed, the land transport modes must employ personnel who understand maritime transportation, and vice-versa, before a more harmonious attitude can emerge. Any lack of cooperation between transport modes only works against the intermodal concept. A particular area in need of strengthening, for example, is the coordination between railways and truck operators. The few acquisitions of trucking companies by railroads in the United States do not indicate full cooperation between these modes. In some regions, the local drayage industry is in great difficulty, with no other mode stepping forward to bail it out. The strength of the total-transport-system concept, it must be remembered, is measured against its weakest link.

Another problem facing intermodality is related to the question of whether this concept can diffuse among all maritime nations. It is clear that many of the developing countries that have resisted containerization will act accordingly toward intermodality, and for the same reasons — roads and rail networks being far from a stage at which they can accommodate a continuous, efficient flow of containers. The developing countries are lagging behind considerably in their adoption of the earlier phase of development-containerization. Efforts to join the containerization era were primarily concentrated on improvements to their seaports. With the chronic financial problems of the developing countries, adoption of intermodal requirements along the entire transport chain is still remote. Furthermore, even if their transport networks were adequate, very few of these economies could afford new investments in facilities and rolling stock, let alone switch from labour-intensive industries to the capital-intensive transport industry. The line of unemployed people in these countries is already very long. The segregated transport industry and unimodal transport services are still the dominant organizational structure in the developing countries.[8]

Within the developed world, too, intermodality does not advance everywhere at the same smooth pace and direction. In Europe, the trend to maintain the ISO container system and the single-stack trains continues, while the United States exhibits an increasing tendency towards longer, higher containers and double-stack container trains. Despite all the difficulties and doubts, however, the level of commitment by many, if not most, of the transport elements to intermodality indicates that the concept has passed the point of no return. Intermodality is plainly here to stay. The chapters that follow attempt to substantiate this statement.

---

8. For further references on the state of containerization in the developing countries, see: Hughes, C. (1977), "Containerization in an LDC Environment", *Maritime Policy and Management* 4, pp. 293–302; *Containerization and the Developing World*. Proceedings of international conference on the growth of containerization and its impact on the economies of developing countries, London, 6–7 October 1980; and current publications of UNCTAD on the subject.

CHAPTER 3

Intermodality in practice

Intermodality as a transport concept experienced substantial development during the early 1980s. Hesitations over accepting the new concept resemble the experience with containerization some twenty years ago, when ports and shipping lines were reluctant to part with their conventional equipment and operating methods. It did not take long, however, for the major participants of the transport industry to understand that adopting containerization had become a matter of necessity and survival rather than just the trial of another technique. As with the "box", criticism and the highlighting of problems can be heard with the new concept; however, the advance of intermodal transportation indicates quite clearly that intermodality is gaining momentum and more and more acceptance on both the international and domestic trade scenes. It seems that the deep commitment of steamship lines, railroads, and seaports to intermodality, manifested in their investments and operating strategies, has brought these transport modes beyond the point of turning back.

It is clear, too, that for a concept aiming to provide an efficient, cost-effective, origin-to-final-destination, integrated transportation service, intermodality is a more complex means — and debatable concept — than was containerization. This is particularly so with regard to its implementation on a world-wide scale. In the light of fundamental differences in geography, nature of the trade, infrastructure, and government policies in various parts of the world — even between two of the focal points of the new transport concept, the United States and Europe — it is unavoidable that the intermodal practice and strategy adopted by the various parties will differ between regions and sometimes within the same region. Containerization has achieved a high degree of standardization on a global scale in terms of box dimensions despite the variations in container-handling equipment and operations methods. It seems unlikely, though, that intermodality, as practised in various parts of the world, be it North America or Europe, will achieve the same degree of acceptance and commonality. The fundamental merit and basic rationale of the integrated transport system will be shared throughout the transport industry. Each region, however, adds its own flavour and distinction, based on its own characteristics, geographical scale and distances, location of demand and supply centres, and structure and organization of its own transport industry.

Intermodality has become a central issue in the United States transport industry. All transport modes involved in carrying freight, both domestically and internationally, are increasing their involvement in intermodality. Some steamship lines, such as Sea-Land and America President Lines (APL), are organizing inland transport services in cooperation with the railroads; ports are improving their intermodal ship-to-rail transfer facilities; and new intermodal freight stations are being established by ports, railroads, and trucking firms. The railways have introduced new specialized rolling stock and are offering an increasing number of dedicated container train services.

The relaxation since 1980 of the regulatory environment surrounding the United States transport industry has enhanced the development of intermodal movements. In 1983, US railroads alone handled 4.1 million trailer and container movements, a 20 per cent increase over the year before.[1] This volume of intermodal traffic and growth could not have been achieved without promotion and investment by the ocean carriers, without a major change in attitude by the railroads, and without the cooperation and coordination of another vital link in the intermodal chain, the ports.

North of the border, two leading companies — the government-owned Canadian National (CN) and the private-sector Canadian Pacific (CP) (the latter part of Canadian Pacific Inc.) — have had a pioneering role in developing intermodal movements in North America. Both companies own and operate a railway network that crosses the country — in contrast to the United States, where there is still no single coast-to-coast railway system. CN and CP are involved not only in railways; they each have also vast interests and involvement in shipping lines, seaports, trucking firms, and even airlines. Intermodal movements are, almost naturally, an important business for the two

1. Association of American Railroads.

companies, and both their current and planned investments in terminal facilities and rolling stock are a clear indication of that fact. In 1985, Canadian National handled 450,000 TEU and trailers; Canadian Pacific intermodal units in 1985 totalled 350,000 TEU. International intermodal traffic in 1980 accounts for about 15 per cent of all railway freight revenues in Canada.[2]

In Europe, intermodality was to a great extent part of the European approach to containerization from the late 1960s on, with containers and trailers being used extensively for intermodal transport. Intercontainer, an organization formed in 1968 and consisting of representatives of 25 European national railroads, coordinates international container movements in Europe. It estimated that in 1985, European trains hauled about 5.4 million TEU, of which more than 80 per cent represented domestic transportation. Inter-container itself handled in 1985 more than 900,000 TEU of international movements, 10 per cent more than the previous year. Some 57 per cent of this traffic consisted of imported or exported maritime containers, and the rest inter-European traffic (including the less than three per cent traffic with the Soviet Union).[3]

GEOGRAPHY AND INTERMODALITY

The implementation of intermodal transport may vary with differences in the basic settings and conditions. With containerization, changes were primarily technological in nature, and, consequently, the diffusion of standardization in terms of cargo-handling equipment or container dimensions was fairly smooth. This was true particularly in the developed world, but also in many countries in the developing world. With containerization, too, the micro scale was rather significant. What difference would it make if the size of a country was small or large or its population density low or high when a decision had to be taken with regard to the purchase of a gantry crane for a given port? Intermodality, on the other hand, by its very nature more

2. Marwick, Peat and Partners (1980), *Intermodal Transportation for Containers and Trailers* (Ottawa: Canadian Transport Commission).

3. Stone, B. (1986), "European Containerization, a Case History", *World Ports*, 49, 3, pp. 37 – 40.

comprehensive, preaches a total concept; thus, a macro viewpoint is more appropriate. Moreover, the emphasis of intermodal transport is on the organizational and logistical dimensions of transport movement; therefore, this concept is highly correlated with the geographical setting and spatial organization of the region or continent.

In North America, the vast areas, long travel distances, and dispersion pattern of the population and industrial centres all have an immediate, direct reflection in the organization and infrastructure of the transport industry. The use of unit trains, double-stack rail container cars, and 40-foot containers are perhaps more attractive in the United States because these elements are designed to achieve improved economies on long-haul movements; indeed, the 40-foot container dominates the United States intermodal scene.

Europe, or more precisely the European Community alone, accommodates a population almost 50 per cent larger than that of the United States in an area nearly one fourth the size of the latter. Distances between large cities in Europe, as well as between the major production centres, and between the seaports and the hinterland are much shorter than in the United States. It is not surprising, then, that the implementation and practice of intermodality take different directions in Europe than they do in North America. The European road and rail networks are much more dense, a reflection of the population-distribution pattern. Flexibility and frequency of service receive more attention from shippers and consignees than do economies of the long-distance haul; thus, the dominance of the 20-foot container in the European intermodal scene has its merit. The European geographical setting also dictates a different competitive arena for transport modes from that in the USA. In Europe, railroads must, and do, strive harder to gain a competitive advantage over trucks on the relatively short distances that characterize the average journey within the continent.

Finally, differences in geopolitical structure between Europe and North America have their impact on the practice of intermodality. The politically segmented European mosaic, defined by the border lines of 25 countries and a complexity of rules and regulations at each one of them, seems almost to contradict one of the basic notions of intermodality — the continuous flow of goods throughout the journey. The customs inspection of trains at the border, which slows down freight movement, stands in contrast to unit trains in the United States, which were created to ensure a fast, smooth journey, in part by avoiding any slow-down and congestion at the conventional switching yards.

In other parts of the world, geography may be counted among the prime factors behind the development of intermodal activities. This is certainly the case with the Mexican landbridge, and it is also an important consideration in the operation of landbridges in the Middle East (see Chapter 6).

RAIL INTERMODALITY

As with containerization, the initiators and promoters of intermodality were the steamship lines. It is only fair to state, however, that the level of development of intermodal traffic greatly depends on the attitude of the railways towards this transport concept. Despite the efforts of container-line operators to enhance intermodality and through-transport rates since the early 1970s, the results of intermodality were rather meagre as long as the railroad industry was reluctant to enter the intermodal arena actively and with a positive attitude.

The growth of intermodal traffic in the United States could not have been achieved without the major change in attitude by the railroads. Evidence of steamship-rail cooperation in that country can be found by the end of the nineteenth century. A certain form of "piggyback" transportation was seen in the United States in the early 1950s; and unit trains were actually in operation well before the emergence of the containerization concept, but with bulk commodities only. Nevertheless, American railways were very slow to adapt themselves to containerization and intermodality. They showed themselves to be very cautious when it came to committing themselves to moving containerized cargo overland: their main interest, and investment, was in bulk commodities. Only in the early 1980s did the US railroad industry finally make the move, and the railway map of America has since changed radically. Deregulation, mergers, new equipment, a systems concept approach, and, what is most significant to the topic of this discussion, increased cooperation with ports and shipping lines — these elements have reformed the development of the US railroad industry in the eighties.

Perhaps the most profound, even inspiring, effect on American railroads stemmed from the deregulation of the industry with the Straggers Rail Act of 1980, which, among other things, covered two intermodal movements, "trailer-on-flatcar" (TOFC) and "container-on-flat-car" (COFC). Until 1980, the strict regulatory policy regarding the transportation industry proved a major constraint for the development of a truly intermodal transportation system. Early attempts to publish through-transport rates were always confronted with the threat of legal action under the anti-trust laws. Neither the Interstate Commerce Commission (ICC) nor the Federal Maritime Commission (FMC) would approve intermodal agreements because of jurisdictional disputes. Then in 1980 the Motor Carrier Act was passed and the possibilities for intermodal transportation in the United States were greatly enhanced. After a century of regulation, the railway industry that year too finally became free to negotiate rates without government control and a new era of competition was entered. With the relaxation of railway and truck regulations covering route selection, type of service, and rates, shippers were introduced to a variety of transport options and to a range of modes, rates, and itineraries.

In Europe, attempts to advance the intermodal movement of cargo in inland transportation came shortly after the introduction of containerization to the continent. In the United Kingdom "Freightliner", an intermodal train, made its debut in the mid-1960s. It was originally designed to handle mainly domestic traffic over short and medium distances and it was supported by an extensive network of terminals throughout the United Kingdom. Despite substantial investments in the system, the fast and frequent service it offered, the Freightliner has failed to attract traffic, particularly for short-distance hauls on which segment trucks have remained dominant.

In continental Europe, intermodal transport was primarily initiated to serve international trade between the seaports and inland centres. During its first decade of operation, intermodal transport developed at a rather slow pace in the light of the relatively short-distance hauls involved, advances of trucking companies, government restrictions on cross-border movements, and quota systems. The late 1970s began to see an improved attitude toward intermodal transportation by a range of governmental and inter-European organizations, including the Council for European Communities and the European Conference of Ministers of Transport. As of the time of writing, the formation of Intercontainer by European railways has had far-reaching consequences, proving to be the most effective organization for dealing with and developing intermodal transportation throughout Europe.

Inland transportation of intermodal traffic is by no means a monopoly of the railroads. Both other veteran modes of freight transportation, such as the motor carrier, and even relatively new modes like the container barge are gradually carving out their niches in the intermodal transport business. The trucking industry was in certain cases even quicker to respond to the new challenge than were the railroads. In the United States, trucking was deregulated in the same year that the railroads were. The Motor Carrier Act of 1980 ended a long period of strict regulation. It removed such restrictions on highway freight transportation as the requirement to obtain permission to operate on specific routes and limitations on consolidation and pooling agreements; it did away with governmental rate control, and it relaxed entry requirements into the trucking business.

With intermodality and a relaxed transport environment, truck companies have also been exposed to competition outside their own mode, as well as within. It was not a great surprise that the exposure to competition drastically brought down transport rates, which in turn induced new businesses to join the industry. The motor carrier industry, however, did not overcapacitize or vanish; on the contrary, it even strengthened its position in certain areas, depending on the region and the market characteristics. Furthermore, competition resulted in a much more significant, long-range impact. Trucking firms began to search for means of greater efficiency and improved productivity and the provision of innovative services. They re-examined their operations to discover weaknesses as well as areas in which they might obtain a relative advantage. As the characteristics of the market place changed with intermodal transportation, some firms responded by merging with each other in order to expand their markets; others increased cooperation with railroads through piggybacking and other services. The use of high-cube, 48-foot containers may even have given trucks an edge over the railroads, which handle ISO containers (20 ft or 40 ft long, 8 ft wide × 8½ ft high). In Europe, intermodality did nothing to erode the competitive edge that truck operators had on short and, sometimes too, on medium-range intermodal hauls.

DOUBLE-STACK RAIL CONCEPT

The first few years following the deregulation of the railroads in the United States witnessed many steps toward a more rationalized, efficient industry. A wide range of new equipment was introduced, among which was a new breed of railroad car built exclusively for container movements. Perhaps the most visible change in the United States railroad industry was the phenomenon of the double-stack container train. The early trials of double-stack train cars were made in 1980 by the Southern Pacific Railroad and American Intermodal. The innovation took a few years to catch hold, but from 1984 exploded over railroad systems throughout the country. By early 1986, over 30 dedicated double-stack trains were hauling containerized freight over long distance routes on a weekly basis (Figure 3).

The double-stack concept received enthusiastic support from American President Lines and then from Sea-Land, and is now being used by more than 10 US and foreign container operators. By using their own dedicated double-stack unit trains, carrying 400 TEU per train, shipping companies can extend the economies of scale achieved with their large container vessels deep into the interior. The shipping lines can, for example, achieve better utilization of equipment and rolling stock by concentrating a high volume of traffic in selected corridors. Moreover, it is apparent that double-stack unit trains can save from 30 – 40 per cent in transport costs per container, compared with conventional TOFC and COFC trains. Finally, the combination of a mother-ship calling at a limited number of ports, the exploitation of the "load centre" concept, and the double-stack container train brings the intermodal concept a major step forward towards fulfilling its goal of a more efficient total transport service.[4]

4. On the load centre concept, see Chapter 5.

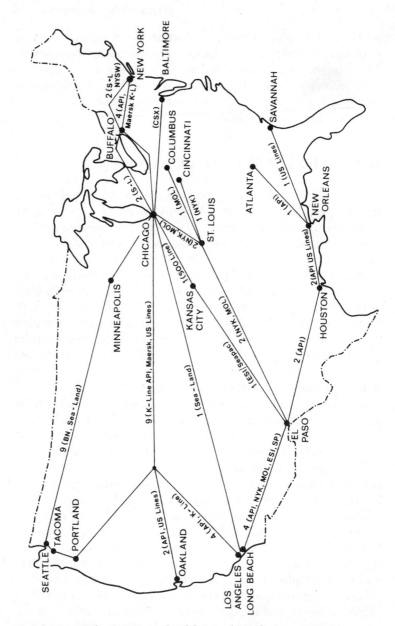

Figure 3. United States double-stack rail connections
Source: *Containerisation International*, March 1986; and *American Shipper*,
February 1986

Despite the great potential, difficulties also exist for the double-stack concept in the United States. The unbalanced trade, greatly in favour of eastbound movement, is a severe marketing problem; the high clearance needed for the double-stacked cargo presents a problem on several routes; and the great dependence of the specialized unit trains on ship scheduling and arrival time has obvious problems.

Nevertheless, it was estimated in the middle of 1986 that the annual capacity of the double-stack units that year would surpass the one million TEU mark. Most of the large US train operators, like Union Pacific, Burlington Northern, Southern Pacific, CSX, Santa Fe, and Norfolk Southern, are heavily involved in the operation of double-stacks at the service of steamship lines. American President Intermodal (API) is currently the largest operator of dedicated double-stack trains, running at least 14 departures a week from the West Coast to the Mid-West and the same number westward. Sea-Land and US Lines follow close behind.

Double-stack container rail-cars were introduced to service individual steamship lines. Necessarily this meant the large lines, and that left in the cold the smaller and medium-sized container lines, which could not guarantee a high volume of containers at a reasonable frequency. Late in 1985, Burlington Northern offered a flexible daily service of common-user double-stack cars as a direct solution of this problem, a solution that has received serious consideration from other railroads as well. Another diversion from the beginnings of the concept is related to route configuration. When a regular double-stack service came on stream in early 1984 on the West Coast – Mid-West trade route, the trains used the ports of Seattle, Oakland, Los Angeles, and a little later Tacoma and San Francisco as their western railheads; Chicago, as the major Mid-West centre. Slightly more than a year later, double-stack services were being offered in new directions: a Los Angeles – Houston link supported by API; a Savannah – New Orleans – Houston service based on traffic generated by US Lines.

Will the double-stack concept be adopted in Europe, as well? It is most unlikely to expect that this phenomenon will diffuse and develop in Europe in the near future; the reasons lie in geography, network characteristics, and demand patterns. The electrification of most of the main tracks in Europe, the many low bridges, and tunnels do not allow the clearance required by the double-stack cars, although the United Kingdom and Scandinavia have more favourable network conditions in this respect. In addition, the economies and advantages of the double-stack concept can best be exploited on high-volume, long-distance corridors, conditions that are very difficult to achieve in Europe, where the average distance for freight hauling is counted in hundreds of kilometres and not in several thousands as in the United States. Lastly, the severe competition between European seaports, which are located within a fairly condensed distance from each other and which have a common hinterland, make it very difficult to create the high volume, let alone the long-distance corridors, to support the efficient operation of dedicated double-stack container trains in Europe.

RAIL MERGERS AND COOPERATION

The intermodal concept, which argues for the continuous and through movement of cargo, was confronted with a fragmented inland transportation scene in both Europe and the United States. In Europe, despite cooperation among states, each country owns a national railroad system with its own policies, regulations, and level of priorities. In the United States, the fragmented railroad industry is of a different nature, consisting of individual privately-owned companies, each one dominating a different region or corridor. None of the railroad systems in the United States can offer a single cross-country service. Any coast-to-coast service, including the minibridge operation, requires either changing equipment at interface locations between different railroad systems or intense cooperation and agreement. This situation in Europe and the United States — unlike that in Canada, where two nation-wide railroad systems operate — is a major obstacle for the further development of intermodal cargo movements overland.

An attempt to overcome Europe's nationally segmented railroad industry was made by establishing the Intercontainer Organization, which coordinates all cross-border container movements and quotes single rates covering the separate rates charged by the individual railway systems taking part in the journey. Intercontainer also operates hundreds of inland container terminals, where the interface between rail and road transportation is effectively handled. The operation of Intercontainer was a great relief from the intermodal point of view; however, the fragmented nature of the railroad industry did not completely vanish, particularly in the light of the nationally oriented policies of the individual member countries, often dictated by governments, and the competition between countries to ensure a greater share of the business for their own seaports.

The advance of intermodality in selected corridors in the United States has enhanced the tendency to merger among US railroads in order to enable them to offer continuous, more efficient movements over longer routes and wider networks. This tendency is yet another important outcome of deregulation. Although not a new phenomenon, the mergers since 1980 added extensive geographical areas to the new railways. The Interstate Commerce Commission (ICC) approved the consolidation of the Union Pacific, Missouri Pacific, and Western Pacific to form the 21-state, 37,000 kilometre-long Pacific Rail System Inc. The Chessie, based in Baltimore, merged with Lines System, based in Jacksonville, to produce a 43,000-kilometre network known as CSX and covering most of the area east of the Mississippi. The anticipated merger between Southern Pacific and Santa Fe and the planned take-over of Conrail by Norfolk Southern will certainly provide two more vastly extended railroad systems, one in the US southern corridor and the other in the East Coast seaboard region. The consolidation of railway systems allows faster, more efficient train movements with unit trains able to bypass many intermediate terminals, avoiding both the delays and the high cost of interchanging cars.

DOMESTIC VERSUS INTERNATIONAL CONTAINERIZATION

Containerization was introduced by the maritime transportion industry and has served primarily this industry. The inland transportation of international trade and the domestic transportation of commodities developed along two different avenues, which normally did not intersect. Whereas the inland transportation of international containerized trade, in both the United States and Europe, used mostly standard marine ISO containers of 20 or 40 feet, domestic transportation was using TOFC (trailer on flat car) in the United States and the "swap body" in Europe. (See Chapter 6 for a description of these units.) Over the years, a clear distinction built up in the nature of the trade, the traffic and the rates between domestic and international containerization. Attempts at cooperation and coordination by Canadian National, Canadian Pacific and several European companies led to the conclusion, early in the containerization era, that the haulage of a combination of domestic and international containers was not economically feasible. The dimensions of over-the-road containers are significantly larger than standard marine containers, and truck carriers fare better, economically, by carrying the larger domestic containers. The use of ISO containers in domestic trade was limited to particular cases, such as container positioning, and confined to the margins of the trade.

Since the early 1980s new trends have emerged. Domestic containerization began to flourish, particularly in the United States. Three main reasons stand behind this change. First, the shift in the centre of gravity of international trade from the Atlantic Ocean to the Pacific and the consequent development of long-haul inland traffic corridors, along which Far Eastern-origin cargo moves via US West Coast ports to the East Coast and the Mid-West, have created an unbalanced inland transport scene in the United States. The volume of imported east-bound sea-going containers far exceeds the volume of westbound export trade from the East Coast to the Far East. Although this trade pattern is as old as the cross-country movements of containers in the United States, the standard-size marine containers faced an inferior competitive position compared to the higher volumes of common domestic containers. The proliferation of double-stack container rail services, offering 20–40 per cent improved efficiency over conventional intermodal operation, has now made the backhauling of international containers on rail cars more attractive. In addition the introduction of high-cube containers, first 45 feet in length and then 48 feet, has further increased the efficiency of hauling marine

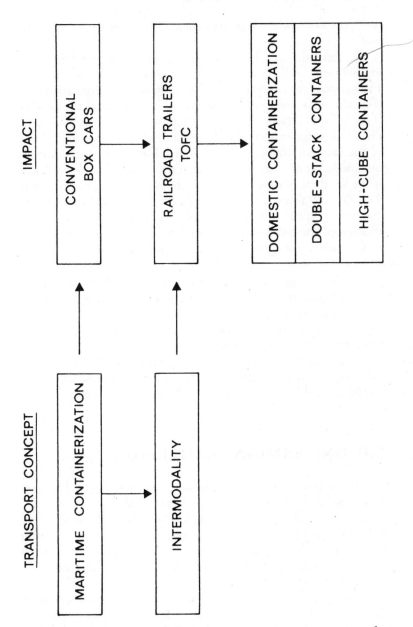

Figure 4. The impact of changing transport concepts on the railways

containers overland, and thus their attractiveness to domestic traffic.

The growth of domestic containerization reveals both competition and complementarity between domestic and international containerization. The growing use in domestic traffic of double-stack, high-cube marine containers comes at the expense of both TOFC traffic to the West Coast and the truck hauliers. This is cause for concern for those railroads that invested heavily in flat cars suitable for TOFC and COFC. They do not eye favourably yet another investment in equipment, but also shudder at the thought of obsolescence. Perhaps ironical is the fact that the railroad trailers that have replaced conventional box cars with the introduction of containerization might be placed in the position of the latter sooner than most people had anticipated, as intermodal transport has promoted domestic containerization, in a process summarized in the schema in Figure 4.

Perhaps unexpected, too, is the fact that with the advent of intermodality, there were early signs of a growing variety of container dimensions (length and height) instead of increased standardization. Additionally, it seems that serious attempts at true intermodal traffic are restricted, to a great extent, to the level of the transport company or shipping line; whereas for shippers searching for greater flexibility, inter-company services, or pooling agreements, the market place is still very much segregated.

THE ON-TERMINAL RAILHEAD

As the volume of intermodal movements increases, it becomes apparent that the transfer of containers from ship to rail and vice-versa remains one of the weakest, least efficent, and most costly links in the intermodal transportation chain. The common practice of off-loading a container onto a chassis, which is then transferred to the rail terminal, often located away from the ocean terminal, is a costly operation in terms of both time and drayage.

It has been obvious since the introduction of containerization that a port that is not accessible to a major railway system is seriously handicapped in the competition for intermodal traffic, but the issue has become even more specific. The distance of the railway terminal from the port is now a critical factor and even a few kilometres in favour of one port over another can prove decisive.

Unlike most European ports, where railheads are commonly located within the port area, US ports generally lack an on-terminal intermodal operation.[5] That most US railway terminals were located away from a port has several possible explanations. There was, first, a certain lack of attention given to this issue when many of the initial container terminals were constructed during the 1960s and the early 1970s. One should bear in mind, though, that in this period steamship lines were preoccupied with introducing the new container vessels, port authorities were confronted with major capital-intensive projects entailing expanding and renovating facilities, and the railroads were altogether reluctant to enter the containerization era. Intermodality was not then at the top of anyone's priority list. Thus the interface operation between ship and rail fell into a "gray area" and very little was done to promote this issue. In addition, at a time when port authorities found themselves badly constrained by the high demand for back-up space for their container terminals, an extra demand for space for the purpose of constructing a rail terminal would not have been welcomed, particularly when the vitality of such a project remained in doubt. The complex relations and agreements between the Longshoremen's Union, responsible for cargo handling within the ports, and the Teamsters, who controlled the work outside the port jurisdiction — the definition of which is a complex issue by itself — was yet another obstacle in the way of joint port-railroad intermodal projects.

The main Santa Fe railway terminal serving the large port of Oakland is located at Richmond, some six kilometres away from the port. The Union Pacific railyard serving the port of Seattle for trains to California is also located at a distance of six kilometres from the port. The Burlington Northern railhead is relocating its facilities from the present terminal, which is about 10 kilometres from the port of Seattle. The situation for the ports of Long Beach and Los Angeles is even worse. Containers moving through one of these ports must bear the cost of first being hauled 40 kilometres

5. Ashar, A. (1984), "Intermodalism, the Case for On-Terminal Operations", *World Ports*, 47, 1, pp. 78–79.

to the nearest Southern Pacific, Santa Fe, or Union Pacific railyard. So significant is the distance of the railhead from the port that two competing neighbouring ports — Los Angeles and Long Beach — are jointly constructing, in conjunction with the Southern Pacific Transportation Company, a major 150-acre Intermodal Container Transfer Facility (ICTF) that will be located just over six kilometres away from their respective marine facilities. Upon its completion, scheduled for the end of 1986, this new facility will cut about 20 million kilometres of truck trips a year from the congested highways of the Los Angeles area, saving both shippers and operators time and expense.

Although some ports on the East Coast, such as Charleston, Savannah, and Wilmington, do operate railhead switching yards within their container terminals, and other ports such as New York and Houston maintain an intermodal terminal very close to the marine facility, there was until recently no on-terminal railhead in operation at any of the West Coast ports, which are heavily dependent on intermodal movements. Several West Coast ports began to consider an on-terminal operation, but the only manifestation of such an intention has come in the Pacific North-West. The willingness of the port of Tacoma to construct an on-terminal container-handling facility is considered one of the main factors behind the decision of Sea-Land, one of the world's largest shipping lines, to have relocated its facilities from the port of Seattle to Tacoma in 1985. Sea-Land was willing to bear the cost of moving its facilities and to incur the additional sailing cost to reach Tacoma because it thought it could improve the ship-to-rail transfer operation and cut existing drayage costs. This single move by Sea-Land not only took away several hundred thousand TEU containers from the successful port of Seattle; it also will upgrade the port of Tacoma to being among the top ten container ports in the United States.

THE AIR-SEA INTERCHANGE

Air freight traffic has grown rapidly over the last decade. The shipment of air cargo has always involved more than one mode of transportation; however, the multimodality was primarily confined to the pick up and delivery of the airborne cargo, usually by trucks going to and from the airports. The consignments consisted in most cases of small parcels and individual shipments. Then, in the past decade, air transportation began to take part in more advanced intermodal movements of cargo on international routes. In fact, a combined sea-air transport service has been offered by both airlines and shipping companies; the shipper thus attains a saving in transport time without paying the high freight that the sole use of air transport would necessitate.

The construction of specially designed intermodal air-surface containers, particularly those measuring 20 × 8 × 8 feet, produced a common denominator for air-sea and air-surface intermodal movements.[6] Early trials with standard sea containers generally proved them too heavy for the aircraft and too expensive for airlines and shippers alike. Now the ability of wide-body jets to accommodate full-size containers in their main deck and the subsequent improvement of ground facilities for freight handling at many airports have enhanced the use of intermodal containers.

An air-sea intermodal service provides shippers with increased flexibility and a wide range of options related to available routes and modes at his disposal, all based on a trade-off between cost and time. A shipper can select, among multiple transport options, the optimal service, ranging from all air to all sea through a combination of air and sea or air and surface modes, according to the shipper's specific needs and fluctuating demand for the product.

Although the precise quantifying of voyage time and costs is greatly dependent on the transport services available on a specific route and the characteristics of the cargo, the trend illustrated in Figure 5 presents an insight into the potential of air-sea intermodal movements. The figure presents the trade-off in transport time and level of freight rates for a delivery from Kobe to Amsterdam with the employment of different transport options. The example refers to a 10,000 pound shipment of television sets (IATA Commodity Code 4416) having an on-deck density of 10 pounds per cubic foot. Of the five alternatives presented in Figure 5, air-sea intermodal service is shorter in time by some two-thirds than an all-water voyage and less in cost by more than half than an all-air journey.

6. For more details of the air mode container design, see: Peak, D. W. (1981), *Developments in the Air Cargo Industry* (London: ICHCA), Ch. 10.

A more up-to-date calculation of the cost and time convergence for shipments along a similar route, from Tokyo to Amsterdam made by Martinair of the Netherlands, again illustrates the potential savings in time and cost of the air-sea intermodal concept.[7] According to this calculation, a direct one-day flight represents a cost level of 100 per cent; a combined sea-air service, via Hong Kong, takes 7–8 days but incurs a relative cost level of 46 per cent; a sea voyage from Tokyo to Seattle across the Pacific and then an air service from Seattle to Amsterdam takes between 13–15 days, about two weeks shorter than the all-water service but entailing a total transport cost only one third of the all-air service. (On the competitive aspects of air freight, see Chapter 8.)

Yet another angle at which to observe the greater involvement of the air transport mode in intermodality is that of the vertical integration of some airlines in the total transport system. American Airlines and Flying Tigers moved into the forwarding field and are providing door-to-door services, using trucks under their control.[8]

7. Gray, T. (1986), "Why Sea-Air Concept is Taking Off", *Lloyd's List*, November 14, p. 5.

8. Mahoney, J. H., (1985), *Intermodal Freight Transportation* (Westport: ENO Foundation for Transportation, Inc.).

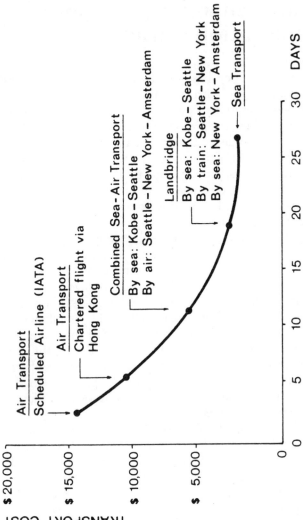

Figure 5. Time and cost trade-off for air-sea and land-sea combined transport services
Source: "Air/Sea Link for Freight Transport", Boeing, 1977.

CHAPTER 4

Structural changes in shipping and international trade

Intermodal transportation has presented shipping lines involved in the container trade with a major challenge. This is the need to pursue operations beyond traditional, sea-orientated responsibilities. Indeed, the profound structural changes that the container shipping industry underwent in the early 1980s was to a great extent a result of the emergence of intermodal transport concepts. Other factors, more general in scope, have combined with intermodality to alter some of the traditional functions of a shipping company and to modify some of the conventional methods of their operation.

For almost half a decade, the container shipping industry has been frustrated by declining freight rates and a vicious circle of overtonnaging. This trend, obviously brought on by fierce competition, is almost a direct result of the prolonged worldwide recession; but the fact remains that while the gross tonnage of container vessels increased by over 60% (from 11.27 million gross tons to 18.4 million) between 1980 and 1985,[1] the volume of containers carried rose by only eight per cent during the same period.[2] Burdened by the high costs of newly built vessels and "rewarded" with reduced revenues, many shipping lines had to rationalize their operations and search for innovative ideas in order to survive the competition.

One trend that stems from these conditions is the constant decline of the national-flag fleets of the countries of the Western World and a shift by this tonnage to flags of convenience in order to fight against the high cost of national crews, heavy taxes, and restrictive regulations.[3] On January 1, 1981, the combined merchant fleet of Europe amounted to some 247 million

1. Lloyd's Register of Shipping, *Statistical Tables*, 1980, 1985.
2. Peter, J. H. (1986), *Trends in Global and Pacific Trades and Shipping* (Bremen: Institute of Shipping Economics and Logistics).
3. Fleming, D. K. (1986), "Safe Harbours", *Maritime Policy and Management*, 13, 1, pp. 17–25.

deadweight tons. By January 1, 1986, a scant five years later, this fleet had shrunk by more than 37 per cent to 155 million deadweight tons. In the two-year period between 1.1.84 and 1.1.86 alone, the European fleet declined by 25 per cent. The flags of convenience, in contrast, have continued to grow, despite the massive scrapping of large tankers. The flags of convenience share of the world fleet reached 30.8 per cent as of 1.1.86 (see Table 1). Another means that shipowners employed to lessen the cost per slot was to increase the size of their vessels. The significance of the introduction in 1985 of the jumbo container vessel of 4,482 TEU capacity went beyond the cost-per-slot objective. It even went beyond the arguments in the industry about the validity of this move by US Lines. The essential fact is that the decade-long restriction of container vessels to the 3,000 TEU size was broken. Other shipping lines are now being induced to order very large container vessels. The proportion of fully cellular container vessels of 2,500 TEU and above increased from 15.7 per cent in 1984 to 21.5 per cent in 1985; further growth is ensured, given the impressive, confirmed orders for this size range.[4] American President Lines' order in 1986 of Panamax Plus container vessels certainly accords with the trend towards larger container vessels; it also marks a new era in containerization: these vessels will be the first containerships not able to transit the Panama Canal.

Table 1. Total world fleet by flag, 1984 – 1986

Flag	Fleet DWT (million tons) 1.1.84	% of world total	Fleet DWT (million tons) 1.1.86	% of world total
Flags of convenience	187.9	29.9%	190.4	31.4%
European countries	202.3	32.2%	155.0	25.6%
Developing countries	95.1	15.2%	101.0	16.7%
Arab countries	17.2	2.7%	12.3	2.0%
Comecon	37.2	5.9%	39.3	6.5%
Others	87.6	14.1%	108.0	17.8%
Total	627.3	100%	606.0	100%

Source: *Shipping Statistics* (Bremen: Institute of Shipping Economics and Logistics).

4. *Containerization International Yearbook*, 1985, p. 14.

Another change, this time regulatory in nature, directly impacts on the development of the intermodal concept, on the one hand, and on structural changes in the shipping industry, on the other hand. On June 18, 1984, after almost a decade of debates, a completely new shipping law, the US Shipping Act of 1984, was passed, thus altering regulatory procedures that had prevailed since the Shipping Act of 1916 with regard to international shipping. One effect of the Shipping Act of 1984 was to accelerate the development of intermodal transportation. The Act grants shipping conferences calling at United States ports the right to set intermodal rates; i.e., a single rate covering the costs of the ocean leg, port time, and the land transport segment for a shipment from origin to final destination. Although most shipping rates must still be filed and reviewed by the Federal Maritime Commission (FMC), they will become effective 45 days after filing, unless the FMC finds them anti-competitive and can obtain a court-ordered injunction to block them. In practical terms, the US Shipping Act of 1984 is an act of deregulation. It is also, however, a regulatory act, since it extended the jurisdiction of the Federal Maritime Commission from the traditional ocean transportation scene to the entire range of intermodal services.

The Act has had the effect of promoting a previously existing trend, that of shipping lines exerting a decisive influence on the destiny of individual ports and on the structure of the United States port system in general. The new law allows the shipping line much greater control over the route of containers throughout the entire journey from origin to final destination. Not only may shipping lines now effect the selection of ports of call, the ocean carriers have also been given greater flexibility in choosing the gateway from which they can enter the inland transportation leg.

Because of the short time perspective, it is still difficult to assess the full impact of the US Shipping Act of 1984. Several shipping companies have already lowered their expectations of benefit from the Act, and some have even expressed concern over the greater ability given to large shippers or "third party" organizations to compete with them in the intermodal race.

The process of the weakening of one of the oldest features in liner trade, the shipping conferences, did not start with intermodality. Innovations in the shipping industry, whether steam in the nineteenth century or containerization in the twentieth, have always been subject to criticism, doubts, and arguments by the conferences. Their traditional foundation seems to be shaken each time something new is offered. Although the conference system has experienced many challenges and threats to its existence, containerization, once it became the dominant method of transporting seaborne general cargo, did have a particularly undermining influence. The claim is made in at least one study that with containerization, competition began to intensify to such a degree that in many trades the ability of conferences to survive or to maintain a different price structure came into question.[5] Moreover, the falling prices of container vessels since the end of the 1970s and the relative simplicity and uniformity of container handling compared with handling conventional break-bulk cargo made it easier to enter the container business than was the case during the early days of containerization. The challenges to the conferences, though, are hurled from various directions. The problem of outsiders is one the conferences seem to have learned to live with, although in many trade routes, such as Europe to Far East trade, and the Atlantic trade, the threat that the conferences' share in the market will be below the 50 per cent level is becoming imminent. Air transportation competes fiercely for the "cream" of the trade. Government subsidies to national fleets, protectionism, and the UNCTAD-inspired cargo-sharing agreements rock the conference system's *raison d'être*. Still, the conferences survive.

Intermodality poses its own threat to the concept of the conference in maritime transportation although claims that the intermodal transport system harbours the biggest danger that the conferences ever faced have yet to be substantiated. Perhaps it is the short time perspective that leads to such serious negative evaluation. It is a fact, however, that following the passage of the US Shipping Act of 1984, discussion of the ability of the conference system to survive the changes in the transportation industry and in international trade began to take place openly at various levels. The validity of open and closed conferences in the United States trade and the question of whether the conferences should be banned altogether found themselves on the official agenda of the Federal Maritime Commission.

5. Graham, M. G. and Hughes, D. O. (1985), *Containerization in the Eighties*, (London: Lloyd's of London Press Ltd.), p. 53.

What is the danger that intermodal transportation presents? The conference system has traditionally negotiated rates primarily for ocean-borne trade routes. "Door-to-door" service accompanied by a through rate and one bill of lading certainly does not fall into the traditional practice of the conferences. In order to cover the inland segments of the intermodal movement of a cargo, the conferences would have to stretch their jurisdiction beyond the ports, as many individual shipping companies actually did in their operations. This move, however, would not solve the problem. Through rates for a cargo shipment from one inland origin to another inland destination cover a complex of origin – destination routes that is much more difficult to control than was the isolated ocean portion of the voyage in the pre-intermodal era. The negotiation apart from the conference framework of inland transport rates by its members is not a long-term solution from the conference point of view; on the contrary, it acts to weaken the conferences themselves.

The deregulation of the US maritime industry has affected not only American shipping lines but also anyone that trades with the United States. A large proportion of the international trade of containerized cargo is tied directly or indirectly to the United States. The US Shipping Act of 1984 provides, among other things, a mandatory right of independent action that contradicts the essence of the conventional conferences, which is to bargain for rates collectively. One manifestation of the greater flexibility allowed US shipping companies is the number of service contracts signed with large shippers and shippers' associations. The exact volume of cargo moving under service contracts is not known, but it is by no means a marginal share of the cargo in many conferences. Service contracts have certainly depressed freight rates and further weakened the conferences. Moreover, with large and influential bodies like shipper's associations bargaining for service contracts, a more selective freight rate system is now altering the long-standing conventional rate-making structure based on general tariffs.

Additionally conferences as well as individual shipping lines have to stand up to yet another type of competition, not necessarily a transport company. The US Shipping Act of 1984 gives backing to the development of groups that are generally referred to as middlemen or "third party" organizations. These may include freight forwarders, large shippers, shippers' associations, and non-vessel-owning common carriers (NVOCCs). They bargain with the conferences for volume rates and may even enter into a slot charter agreement with shipping lines. The NVOCCs are of particular concern to the conferences. Unlike most middleman organizations, which are mainly concerned with bargain rates, the NVOCCs actually offer shippers intermodal transport, including door-to-door service of less-than-container-load (LCL) shipments.

GLOBALIZATION OF THE WORLD ECONOMY

The structural changes in the shipping industry are closely correlated with a much wider change that has taken place in the world economy in general and in international trade in particular. Since the 1970s, particularly during the later part of that decade, the traditional structure of the world economy has shifted in a direction that is quite clear — the internationalization of production.[6] The emergence of a global system of production fosters, among other things, an increase in the size of individual firms engaged in production for international trade, certainly an expansion of the spatial scale of their operation. The development of the multi-national corporation is, on the one hand, a significant outcome of this trend: on the other hand, it is a major catalyst for the process of production on a global scale. Multinational development means more than just the addition of foreign subsidiaries to a company in one of the developed countries. It represents, in most cases, a complicated, sophisticated, and highly coordinated production and distribution chain. For example, the selection of a specific location for a plant of such a corporation is based in large measure on the relative advantage of each and every site considered, no matter where on the globe, in terms of capital incentives, labour and transport costs, and accessibility. It is the aggregate locational preference of many multinational corporations that is responsible for the shifts in international trade. Vertical integration and external economies, which constitute two of the fundamental bases of the

6. Taylor, M. and Thrift, N. (eds.), *The Geography of Multinationals* (London: Croom Helm).

multi-national corporation, could not have been achieved, however, without reliable, low-cost ocean transportation and advanced information systems.[7]

The globalization of the economy has other connotations as well. It is generally considered to be synonymous with the industrialization of the developing countries, the deindustrialization of the developed states, and the expansion of service industries to a global scale.[8] Indeed these three processes directly bear on the changing structure of international trade, and the trade balance between countries, and consequently on the shipping industry as a whole.

Table 2. Value of imports and exports of all trade, by regions, 1966 – 1982 (%)

	1966	1970	1974	1978	1982
Developed					
Countries	69.42	71.83	68.04	67.78	64.69
North America	17.74	17.59	15.92	15.84	15.57
Europe	43.79	45.15	42.48	42.98	39.43
South Africa	0.95	0.95	0.69	0.59	0.70
Asia[(*)]	4.92	6.30	7.30	7.02	7.48
Oceania	2.02	1.84	1.65	1.35	1.51
Developing					
Countries	19.24	17.70	23.04	22.55	25.65
Africa	3.99	3.72	4.08	3.94	3.94
Central and					
South America	6.30	5.67	6.15	5.36	5.63
Asia	8.73	8.06	12.60	13.07	15.92
Others	0.22	0.25	0.21	0.18	0.16
Socialist					
Countries	11.34	10.47	8.92	9.67	9.66
Eastern Europe	9.97	9.54	7.85	8.73	8.46
Asia	1.37	0.93	1.07	0.94	1.20
World total	100.00	100.00	100.00	100.00	100.00

[(*)]Japan and Israel.
Source: UNCTAD, *Yearbook of International Commodity Statistics*, 1984.

7. Casson, M. (1983), *The Growth of International Business* (Boston: George Allen & Unwin).

8. On multi-national development of the service industries, see: Heskett, J. L. (1986), *Managing in the Service Economy* (Boston: Harvard Business School Press), Ch. 8.

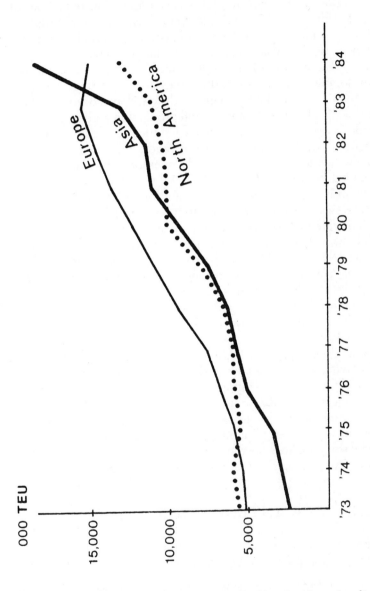

Figure 6. Volume and containers handled by the three leading regions in the world
Source: *Containerisation International* and Author's Questionnaire

   Developed countries, in their search for possible reductions in production costs, have relocated considerable labour-intensive production activities to developing countries. From their point of view, the latter saw this move as a major employment opportunity; but an attendant result proved to be an increase in the developing world's share of the total value of international trade compared with a relative decline of the developed countries' share (Table 2). The growth of industrial production and international trade were particularly concentrated in the Pacific basin countries: Taiwan, South Korea, Hong Kong, and Singapore. Asia's share in the world international trade, measured by value, almost doubled between 1966 and 1982.

   In addition to this spatial redistribution of international trade, as measured by value, the shift in international trade directions is illustrated also by the volume of cargo. In 1973, 17 per cent of the world's container traffic was handled in Asia; this rose to 29.6 per cent in 1984. During the same period, Europe's share of the container traffic dropped by 7.4 per cent.[9] By the mid-1980s, in fact, Asia was the world's largest continent in terms of container handling (Figure 6); and seven of the twelve largest container ports in the world were located in the Far East and South East Asia.[10]

   The globalization trend, as seen, led to a shift in the centre of gravity of the containerized trade from the Atlantic to the Pacific Ocean. The shift affects not only the deployment of containership capacity but also the very container industry, with a growing control of this sector being concentrated in the Far East in terms of shipbuilding and container slot ownership. In 1985, shipping lines operating from Far East countries controlled more than 25 per cent of the world container slot capacity.

VERTICAL INTEGRATION

Intermodal transportation has encouraged shipping lines to break away geographically and functionally from their conventional task

   9. *Containerization International Yearbooks*, personal questionnaires, and correspondence.
   10. Hong Kong, Kaoshiung, Kobe, Singapore, Yokohama, Keelung, and Busan, in declining order.

of transporting ocean-going trade between ports. During the early stages of containerization, the container-vessel operator pursued activity beyond the ports mainly to control inventory — the containers — and to ensure that the boxes were returned once the client discharged the cargo. When shipping lines recognized that intermodal transportation was not just a temporary method of hauling cargo, but a method of transport that was here to stay, they also learned that on many trade routes, the proportionate cost of the ocean voyage in the total transport cost from origin to destination was rather small, both relatively and absolutely. Consequently, some ocean carriers have changed their passive attitude to involvement in the inland transport segments. They have three motivations for taking this step, some companies having done so with a heavy foot: first, to ensure traffic for themselves on the ocean voyage leg; second, to seize a fair share of the expanded inland transport market that has been opened up to them; and third, to establish their own role in the intermodal transport chain.

A firm can at times increase its scale of operations simply by enlarging its plant size. It can also expand by controlling, through vertical integration, the functions and activities that are linked either in forward or backward direction to their part in the production process. In an extreme form, for example, a firm may control the production of raw materials, the manufacturing of a product, and its distribution to the customers. In the same manner, shipping lines have started, particularly since 1980, to assume greater control through vertical integration of larger portions of the total distribution of cargo.[11] Although container lines have participated in the overland movement of their cargo for some years, the advance of intermodal transport has accelerated the involvement of shipping in land transportation. Shipping lines have developed close cooperation and partnerships with railways, trucking companies, large freight forwarding firms, inland container depots, and intermodal freight stations.

The railway–steamship partnership is amongst the most remarkable changes in the current development of intermodality.

11. On the situations that promote or discourage vertical integration, with implications for shipping, see: Casson, M. (1986), "The Role of Vertical Integration in the Shipping Industries", *Journal of Transport Economics and Policy*, XX, pp. 7–29.

During the 1960s and throughout most of the 1970s, railroads were reluctant to commit themselves to any agreement with container shipping operators. Then in the early 1980s, as trans-continental traffic grew with the deregulation of the railway industry, the door was opened to mutual cooperation. Railway—steamship alliances have produced significant trunk routes in the United States. Sea-Land, American President Lines, and US Lines began channelling their Far East containers by means of dedicated unit trains, each shipping line in its own corridor, from the Pacific North-West to Chicago and New York, from Southern California to the Mid-West and the South, and from the San Francisco Bay area to Chicago. Some of the shipping lines, like APL and Sea-Land, own and operate double-stack trains, specialized rail cars designed by the shipping lines themselves. In the light of these developments, it seems almost inevitable to expect the purchase of a railroad system by a container shipping line. Indeed, this move has come, but in a reverse direction — a railway is planning to buy a containership company. CSX, a railroad giant and the dominant corporation in the eastern part of the United States rail transport system, is expecting approval of its take-over bid for Sea-Land, one of the largest containership operators in the world. The merger of CSX and Sea-Land, each with its own strong segment of the transport chain, would mean the effective formation of a huge intermodal transport company. CSX could coordinate its rail-service schedules with Sea-Land's calls, and both companies would benefit from the traffic generated by the other.

It is interesting that thirty years ago, Sea-Land was primarily a trucking firm, which then moved into the shipping business as one of the major promoters of containerization. Now, it finds itself negotiating its future role in the intermodality business with an inland transport mode. Throughout the containerization era and during the early phase of intermodality, it was the container lines that were the most innovative among the transport modes. The attempt by a railway to buy a container line represents more than a diversion from this trend; it illustrates the recognition by inland transport modes of the current importance and future potential of intermodality.

The significance of the CSX—Sea-Land case, whether the merger is approved or not, goes beyond the two companies directly involved. The projected unification represents a growing trend in international freight transportation to create a supermarket-type company, in which the shipper can find a full range of transportation and distribution services under one corporate roof; there will be no need for separate and multiple negotiations in order to transfer goods from origin to final destination. In other words, this trend signifies strong interest in the formation of multi-modal or total-transport companies.

In North America, Canadian Pacific Corporation (CP) and Canadian National (CN) have in fact been multi-modal companies for quite some time. They operate land, sea, and air transport services, supported by inland container depots and distribution services.[12] In Europe, the phenomenon of a multi-modal company is also familiar. Hapag-Lloyd, in addition to its fleet of vessels, also owned and operated aviation and freight forwarding activities before 1980. The creation of a multi-modal company in the United States in the 1970s was prevented not only by economic constraints, but primarily by regulatory restrictions. Under then-existing transport regulations, mergers within or between modes were almost impossible. When most regulations were lifted in the early 1980s and the economic rationale for forming large multi-modal transport companies was substantiated, structural changes began to take place in individual transport companies. Shipping lines involved in intermodal transportation, as well as railroads, started to buy trucking companies, inland terminal operations, and freight forwarding agencies. Such moves are justified from both the economic and marketing perspectives. A multi-modal company can potentially distribute cargo among the various modes under its control with better coordination and improved efficiency in comparison with the operation of a segmented transport mode. A total transport company can cut duplicate administrative expenses and combine marketing efforts. With the consolidation of various modes under one managerial umbrella, such a company can, again, potentially benefit from the relative strengths that each mode brings from its own region, area of speciality, and traditional customers.

Significantly, the changing perspectives of shipping lines, from seeing themselves merely as ocean carriers to becoming multi-

12. Marwick, Peat and Partners (1980), *Intermodal Transportation for Containers and Trailers* (Ottawa: Canadian Transport Commission).

modal concerns with involvement in trucking, railroading, warehousing, and cargo distribution, represent an alteration of the basic character of the conventional shipping company. With regard to the pace of development of intermodality, it seems inevitable that the establishment of total transport companies, performing a diverse range of activities in transportation as well as in related services and operating with extended geographical coverage, is not just a current trend, it is also a promising future.

RATIONALIZATION

The changing environment of international seaborne trade, the rigid competition on most containerized trade routes, the low freight rates, the limited growth in traffic volume, the imbalance in cargo flows on the major routes, and the need for capital expenditure in order to integrate services in intermodality have all led in one direction — rationalization. Although rationalization generally implies optimization of operation, greater efficiency, and better utilization of resources and equipment, there is more than one way to achieve these goals. Rationalization can occur both within and between shipping lines. It can affect the scale of operation of a shipping line, size of a firm, design of routes and itineraries.

Modern ocean transportation is a very capital-intensive industry. This description is particularly true for container shipping, for which capital investment includes not only the vessel but also the several sets of containers for each ship. As shipping lines add the inland transport segment to their operations, small operators find it increasingly difficult to obtain necessary capital for ship construction, let alone money for additional investment. There is an inevitable tendency towards corporate concentration in the shipping industry, the purpose of which is to widen the capital-raising potential and to share the growing risk. The enlargement of shipping companies through horizontal integration can result in economies of scale for liner shipping operations. Internal economies can be obtained through acquisitions, mergers, or pooling agreements, which both increase the size of a company and combine the operations of several shipping companies and several sequential operations under a common management. The enlarged shipping companies thus gain better control of a larger share of the market and also eliminate certain costs incurred in a segregated operation. In Europe, mergers took place to create Nedlloyd and Hapag-Lloyd, and the merger of American President Lines (APL) with American Mail Line (AML) provides an example from the United States.

Cargo potentials on high-density routes are tempting for many ship operators. The larger, faster vessels are especially attracted to these routes. This results in tough competition and, on many of these routes, excess capacity. Constant efforts are required to provide the large vessels with the necessary volume of cargo so that they may benefit from high load factors. Low load factors have a more damaging effect on expensive container-ships than on conventional liners. This heated competition has forced some shipping lines to go out of business, others to merge, and still others to think about cargo-pooling arrangements and other means of collaboration. The exit of several companies from main routes, however, has been more than offset by the introduction of more sophisticated, larger ships, whose increased productivity adds a burden to the overtonnaging situation.

The cooperation or collaboration of liner operators in consortia and in shipping conferences reflects other, less permanent forms of corporate concentration. The high fixed-cost aspects of the container system tended to encourage such arrangements in the early days of containerization. The same rationale is maintained with intermodality, for which the investment in streamlining operations and in becoming involved in other segments of the total transportation chain is very high; consequently, too, the need mounts to obtain the necessary volumes of cargo. In Europe, the enormous capital cost of setting up a door-to-door container distribution system and the need to replace conventional break-bulk ships with new, expensive containerships have been conducive to cooperative ventures by shipping lines. Thus, Atlantic Container Line (ACL) is an amalgamation of six lines, Associated Container Transportation (ACT) is a consortium of five different lines, and OCL consists of three companies.

Pooling combined resources through joint fleet agreements proved a ready method to rationalize container operations. On the United States – Far East route, six Japanese firms collaborated to operate jointly a large fleet of container vessels; the joint operation of Australia–Europe Container Service (AECS) and Trio, a cooperative operation of British, Japanese, and German shipping companies in the Europe–Far East trade, is an example of this manifestation in a different part of the world.

Yet in the present intermodal era, another form of rationalization is occurring — the slot-charter agreement. The deregulation of the United States shipping industry that came with the US Shipping Act of 1984 eliminated many of the constraints and threats of anti-trust legal claims and thereby allowed shipping lines to collaborate through slot-charter agreements. Such cooperation between shipping lines, which has been in practice for years on many trade routes, has especially flourished since 1985 on United States trade routes. The agreements between Evergreen and Japan Line and between OOCL, NOL, and K-Line are but two instances of arrangements formed on a large scale in 1985 and 1986.

The various forms of rationalization in the shipping industry — mergers, consortia, joint fleets, pooling agreements, slot-charter agreements — possess two common characteristics: concentration and growth in scale of operation. These qualities describe yet another important structural change in liner shipping. A research study dealing with the concentration of capital in shipping and the optimum size of shipping companies concluded that from the 1920s to the 1950s the tendency was to converge towards the medium-size liner shipping company, ranging from 10 to 40 ships; however, during the 1960s and 1970s, when containerization established itself in the liner trade, the average size of shipping companies increased substantially.[13]

Concentration not only characterizes the current structure of the shipping industry at the level of the shipping company, it also marks the main feature of the spatial distribution of the containerized trade. Consequently, the world-wide distribution of container capacity is highly concentrated: excluding intra-regional movements, about 50 per cent in 1980 was concentrated in three trade routes — North America–Far East (20.6%), Europe–North America (19%), and Europe–Far East (9.8%).[14]

13. Swendsen, S. (1978), "The Concentration of Capital in Shipping and the Optimum Size of Shipping Companies", *Geo Journal*, 2, 2, pp. 163–178.

14. Pearson, R. and Fossey, J. (1983), *World Deep Sea Container Shipping* (Liverpool: The University of Liverpool), p. 2.

Moreover, the concentration is also apparent within each route, in that very few shipping lines provide the majority of the capacity in each case.

Employing large container vessels on high-volume routes, carriers have to retain adequate frequency of service if they are to retain their customers. As a result, the carriers prefer a distinct channelling of service, calling at a limited number of ports on each side of the ocean. On the United States Atlantic and Gulf Coasts, there were 30 line-haul ports serving frequent international ocean carriers in 1973. By 1983, the number of such ports had more than halved to 12.[15] An important incentive for consolidating overseas trade routes is the necessity of maintaining a high load factor on the large containerships with their high daily operating costs.

It is interesting to note a parallel development in air transportation. The Airline Deregulation Act of 1978 brought about a structural change in the airline industry in the United States, the environment of free competition causing airlines to rationalize their operations. The most distinct development along this line was the concentration of a carrier's traffic at large air hubs and the formation of "hub and spoke" networks.[16] Air hubbing is an attempt to maintain a high level of aircraft utilization and to take advantage of scale operations.[17] Another advantage that airlines operating under such a concept can gain is the retaining of more on-line traffic under their services and control. This phenomenon certainly bears clear similarity to the trend by shipping lines towards a greater concentration in their sailing network. Moreover, it does produce some interesting reflections on the integration of shipping lines in the intermodal system.

Still another important change in the shipping industry, one with an economic and a spatial flavour, is the adoption of a global strategy in the form of a round-the-world container service. Ignoring the economic stagnation of the world economy, the low

15. Peters, A. J. (1986), *Trends in Global and Pacific Trades and Shipping*, (Bremen: Institute of Shipping Economics and Logistics), p. 6.

16. On this issue, see: Phillips, T. L. (1985), "Structural Changes in the Airline Industry: Carrier Concentration at Large Hub Airports and Its Implications for Competitive Behaviour", *Transportation Journal*, 29, 2, pp. 18–28.

17. Kanafani, A. and Ghobriel, A. A. (1985), "Airline Hubbing — Some Implications for Airport Economics", *Transportation Research*, 19A, pp 15–27.

level of freight rates, and the potential shortage of cargo for their services as an outcome of the UNCTAD cargo-sharing liner code, United States Lines and Evergreen, a Taiwanese shipping line, each launched a dedicated round-the-world service in 1984. United States Lines offered a weekly eastbound service, with twelve new "mammoth" vessels of 4,482 TEU each, in themselves another breakthrough in container liner shipping. Evergreen Lines also scheduled a weekly service but in both eastbound and westbound directions, with 11 G-type containerships of 2,728 TEU each. Both lines, however, ran into subsequent difficulties. US Lines first dropped the ports of Jeddah and Fos from its itinerary late in 1986, leaving only 11 ports on its round-the-world service. Trouble with finding sufficient cargo for these ships and their huge newbuilding costs finally brought the company as a whole to file for bankruptcy. Evergreen Lines, for its part, withdrew from its Europe-to-Middle East service, but continued to call at about 15 ports around the world.

Although these two lines made most of the headlines at the time, others were also operating a global or nearly global service. Barber Blue Sea Line (BBL) ran an eastbound round-the-world service. ABC Containerline offered a round-the-world service via Australia and New Zealand. OOCL jointly with Neptune operated a near global service. Zim, using two different lines, also effectively circumnavigated the globe. Yang Ming was planning to operate a round-the-world service as well.

The initial moves by United States Lines and Evergreen to operate global services attracted much attention in the shipping industry. There was, as might be expected, considerable criticism and scepticism concerning the rationale of such a move, its timing, and its chances of success. The withdrawal in 1986 of portions of the service by both lines, acts blamed on low rates, small cargo volumes, and, for US Lines, financial difficulties, further increased the doubts. Nevertheless, the round-the-world service represents an important stage in containerisation and intermodality.

A global service provides a different approach to rationalization and the restructuring of container liner services. Not only is the spatial scale different, but the long voyage traverses diversified markets, each with different characteristics, sails across well-established trade routes, and confronts the imbalance of trade from a different viewpoint. Round-the-world service with few ports of call depends, to a great extent, on the quality and efficiency of its feeder system. It is feasible to conceive of economies of scale achieved by the large vessels employed on the main routes; but a global service does not stand in isolation. It is as an intermodal service, a total system, including feeder services and inland transport, that it must be evaluated. It might very well be that the operation and costs of the supporting services offset the advantages of the "mother ships".

The round-the-world operations by United States Lines and Evergreen attracted and concerned most containership operators for a variety of reasons. There were the issues of increased capacity in already overtonnaging conditions on many routes and the attendant pressure thus imposed on the level of freight rates. On the other hand, potential savings in costs per slot with the large new vessels were seen as potentially significant. Should the two companies succeed in achieving a high load factor, their competitors would be required to react to the challenge.

The developing countries have voiced mainly concern with regard to the global services.[18] They fear that the competition thereby engendered will undermine their own efforts to penetrate and integrate into the container liner trade as full partners. The inability to compete on a global route could downgrade their national lines to the level of feeders for the principal round-the-world services.

18. For more on the developing countries' point of view, see; United Nations Conference on Trade and Development, *Major Issues in World Shipping, Structure of World Shipping*, Geneva, August 25, 1986.

CHAPTER 5

Seaports and the intermodal chain

The history of port development clearly shows that changes in seaports were largely a reflection of and response to progress in the industries they served, particularly the maritime transportation industry. Innovations in the design of ships and in the technology of loading and discharging vessels and the growing dimensions of ocean carriers were the prime catalysts of port development in the past. Today, seaports are operating in even more complex systems than ever before. Containerization has altered many of the traditional methods of terminal operations, and the emerging integrated, intermodal transport systems have modified conventional port functions and introduced new facets of port competition. Ports are increasingly dependent not only on transportation modes, but also on logistical, marketing and environmental systems. Any analysis of seaports, then, necessarily involves an evaluation of the trends and developments of the elements on which seaports depend.[1] This means that the discussion must focus not only on issues such as future developments in ship technology, but also on marketing strategy, automated information systems, and integrated transportation concepts.

A port is, and always has been, a dependent element of the system within which it operates. The question may be raised: can a seaport continue to be a passive actor and merely respond to external developments as it has done in the past? Or should it break out of the traditional concepts of port planning and development and expand its horizons, so to speak, to become a more active, initiating factor in modern transport and commercial systems? Indeed, there are indications that seaports are going through a period of fundamental change in operational methods, physical layout, organizational structure, and the range

1. Hayuth, Y. (1985), "Seaports: The Challenge of Technological and Functional Changes", in *Ocean Yearbook 5*, E. M. Borgese and N. Ginsburg, eds. (Chicago: University of Chicago Press), pp. 79–101.

of activities in which they are involved. As the intermodal transport concept progresses, ports are struggling to establish their role in the total transport chain.

Containerization and intermodality represent two distinct, although closely related, impacts on seaports. One theme of this book, that intermodal transportation has introduced a second, new phase into the container revolution, certainly has merit with regard to ports.

STAGES OF CHANGE

Containerization, from the port perspective, has been viewed largely in terms of revolutionary technological changes in cargo handling, and quite rightly so. The objective of port containerization, in its earlier stages, was to better the productivity of cargo handling. Born of the need to reduce the turn-around of ships in port, containerization had as one of its main targets the improvement of cargo throughput. Indeed, a major advantage of containerization over conventional cargo-handling systems lies in its ability to transfer cargo at a much faster rate from land to ship and from ship to shore.

New cargo-handling methods and modifications of terminal facilities characterized the entry of ports into the containerization era. In the United States, Europe, and the Far East, the late 1960s and the early 1970s were years in which almost all major ports constructed newly equipped terminals. Large, high-speed gantry cranes, with a lifting capacity of 30–40 tons, replaced the conventional 3–5 ton loading/unloading gear. Various types of straddle carriers became a dominant factor in yard operations, nearly ousting the conventional fork lift, which previously had been given the main burden of sorting and organizing the cargo before its loading or after its discharge. The new equipment, together with the unitization of cargo handling and the construction of specialized terminals, dramatically improved port productivity and transformed the port industry from being labour intensive to capital intensive.[2] Within less than a decade, technological progress in handling cargo in ports transformed the

2. Hoyle, B. S. and Hilling, D. (1984), *Seaport Systems and Spatial Change* (Chichester: John Wiley & Sons).

recurrences of ship congestion and long waiting times to a port-industry characterized by overcapacity.

Since fixed costs are much higher than variable costs in container terminals, it is obvious that a terminal operator will strive to increase throughput. Only a high degree of utilization can justify the large investment required for a specialized container terminal. The optimum throughput of a container terminal, however, varies with different locational factors, operational policies, and competitive environments. Since the terminal depends on its customers, and obviously the ship operator is one of them, any evaluation of terminal capacity must take into account the viewpoints of both the port and the carrier. The ocean carrier favours ports that can provide enough capacity to ensure a fast turn-around time with no delays. Yet this may mean that the facility will be underutilized. On the other hand, port authorities prefer to employ their facilities at the highest rate possible. That, however, may cause congestion and waiting time.

Theoretically, the capacity of any container terminal should be determined as a compromise between these two outlooks, of the port and of the carrier, at the point at which the combined cost of idle facilities and idle ships is the lowest. Practically, however, in a competitive port environment in which a ship operator has a choice of ports at his disposal, ports must ensure the availability of a berth upon a vessel's arrival. As a result, although the technological progress brought about by containerization may have greatly improved cargo handling efficiency in ports, it is also responsible for the overcapacity of terminal facilities in most developed countries.

In addition to the technological changes, the effect of containerization on the conventional port system was manifested in two other avenues of impact: the spatial and the organizational (Figure 7). The improved cargo-handling capabilities of the gantry crane compared with the conventional crane had an immediate impact on the ratio between the length of a berth and the amount of back-up land. Typically, two to three acres of finger piers had delineated the conventional general cargo port. Container-handling being a space-demanding operation, the common size of terminals in most container ports in the 1980s mushroomed to five to six acres. The great demand for back-up space, together with the need to improve accessibility to inland transportation networks, soon necessitated the relocation of terminals — and rendered many port facilities obsolete. Expansion of the port proper was impossible if adjacent areas were already built up or otherwise designated for non-port activities, or if land acquisition costs were prohibitive. Container terminals, often finding it difficult to operate at the existing waterfront port, were then forced to move to the fringe of the urban area, where space was available, or even to relocate to an entirely new location. One way in which port authorities, particularly in Europe, have solved their need for more space is through downstream reclamation — the construction of wide, flat sites and the dredging of deep water alongside. The relocation of port facilities from London's old docks to Tilbury can serve as an example. Other illustrations of this worldwide trend of the shift of the centre of port activities are from Manhattan in New York City to Elisabeth, New Jersey; from Marseilles to Fos; and from Alexandria to Dekahilia in Egypt.

In addition to having a spatial impact, containerization has also altered various organizational aspects of the port industry. The organizational structure of the port hierarchy has been modified by containerization, and several small ports — the port of Oakland serves as a notable example — were raised to the top list of port rankings while other large, usually conventional ports such as San Francisco declined. Containerization has also promoted the core-periphery structure in the port system, as will be elaborated in the latter part of this chapter, and the use of single billing and multi-modal rate agreements. Although these last two features were already evident in the 1970s, one should bear in mind that, in general, the elements of the transportation industry then involved in international trade were to a great extent fragmented in nature and, at least in the United States, strictly regulated.

In innovation diffusion theory, every innovative idea or product has a certain life cycle; when it can no longer be considered an innovation, then in most cases there begins a new cycle of innovations.[3] Port containerization, in its conventional form, seems to have reached a certain degree of maturity by the end of the 1970s. Container terminal operation has been common for more than a decade along the main trade routes of the Atlantic and the Pacific, and the spread of containerization to developing countries has intensified. Ship-to-shore operations have now been

3. Brown, L. A. (1981), *Innovation Diffusion* (London: Methuen).

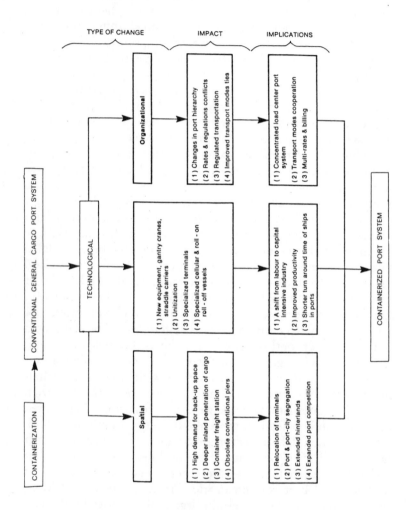

Figure 7. The impact of containerization on the conventional general cargo port system

performed by essentially the same gantry cranes for nearly two decades. No further significant changes in operation can be observed at the terminal back-up area for a decade. The trend of constant improvements in port productivity that characterized so much of the early stages of containerization has greatly moderated. In sum, the once-new containerized port system, which replaced the conventional general cargo port system, is an established fact.

International freight transport in general and the port industry in particular are now embarked on a new phase, a new cycle of innovation, in which containerization has become the common denominator of an emerging intermodal transport concept. Although intermodality is a natural continuation of containerization, the emphasis and focus of the two concepts are not necessarily in the same direction (Figure 8). The first phase of port containerization involved a period of technological change and of massive growth in the spatial dimensions of terminals. The second phase focuses attention on the organizational aspects of international transport and the port industry, on marketing strategies, and on greater participation by ports in the physical distribution of the cargo. Thus in this new phase, ports, too, began to be seen in the light of a total, integrated transport system.

It is quite natural that after implementing massive changes, port managements should seek a period of stability and "relaxation" in order to absorb the changes and harvest some revenue from their investments. For the port industry, however, such a calm period has yet to arrive. The new phase of intermodality was at its doorstep hard on the heels of containerization. With little or no time to digest the technological changes, seaports have had to re-evaluate their functions and operational methods amidst the uncertainties and heat of a changing competitive environment brought on by new developments: relaxation of the transport regulatory environment (particularly in the US), greater cooperation among transport modes, increased involvement by transport modes in one another's traditional "territory", and larger container vessels. The shaken containerized port system had to shift its focus to activities that were essentially organizational in nature. This is not to say that the port industry as a whole neglected the technological aspects of its operations — be they in crane productivity, intermodal facilities, or any other physical mechanism — or that spatial assets, such as improved ship-to-rail accessibility, did not continue to play a role in port development. Rather, predominant attention began to be paid to inland transportation, new marketing schemes, multi-modal rates, improved documentation, computerization, and effective information systems. These logistical-organizational subjects occupy port management in the second, or intermodal, phase of containerization.

THE PORT'S ROLE IN TRANSITION

The role of a port in the transport system is aligned in relation to services performed: for ships, goods, land-transportation modes. If the concept of the transport system is transformed, the probability is that the function of the port will be affected. Containerization and, particularly, the intermodal transport concept effected such a transformation: the port became a rapidly passed point rather than an abrupt break in the end-to-end transport haul. The new concepts altered the traditional role of ports and reduced the importance of some of the conventional waterfront services; they also imparted new functions to the seaports.

Intermodality has forced seaports to stretch their activities and functional responsibilities beyond the traditional port boundaries. In an effort to carve out a position in the intermodal transport system, ports are assuming an expanded role as a central link in the total transport chain, rather than as a terminus or break-of-bulk point in the conventional general cargo trade. Necessarily, ports have always been dependent on transportation elements, which are vital for their existence; however, now there is a difference compared to the past: in the intensity and scale marking the level of cooperation and also in the subject matter. No longer merely responding to changes in related transport elements, ports have gradually been breaking away from their traditional, passive function in transportation and taking a more active, initiative role.

Major ports have always been distribution centres and gateways between hinterland and foreland. In order to benefit from their strategic position in a total transport system, ports have increased their involvement in physical distribution systems. Rotterdam is a prime example. Many ports have started to offer extensive

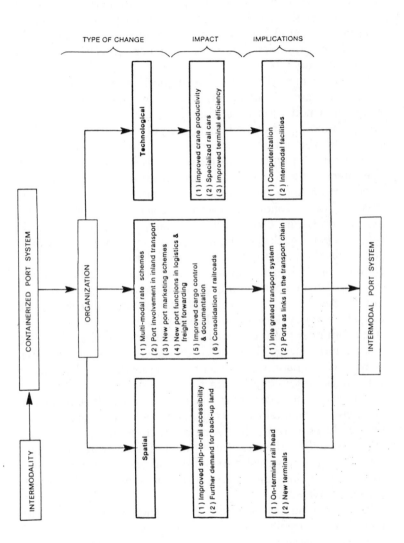

Figure 8. The impact of intermodal transport on the containerized port system

consolidation services to both shippers and shipping lines. Since full container load shipments represent just part of the total container traffic, small consignments of cargo, from different origins and bound for different destinations via the same port, need to be consolidated into full containers in order to save on transport costs.

One of the most significant contributions of these consolidation centres at a port is in advancing high-volume, fast-moving, longer-range intermodal journeys. Fast, large containerships and the speedy handling of containers at the port would by themselves not yield the ultimate advantage of large-scale intermodal movements. A port consolidation centre helps to extend, far into the interior, the economies of scale from the concentration of goods into a single linear flow. For all practical purposes, ports involved in consolidation services are acting as transportation agents and freight forwarders. For example, the port of Seattle offered a package deal to small shippers in which the port would not only be responsible for consolidating the cargo and transferring containers from ship to railroad, it would also arrange inland movements, including documentation. So much has the port of Seattle become involved in the physical distribution of cargo that it provides eastbound container booking for the double-stack container trains operated by Burlington Northern between Seattle and Chicago. The port further offers train-load planning, drayage coordination, container-trucking services, and assistance with marketing in the Far East.

Obviously, not every port can engage in activities related to the logistics of container movements. Some ports are constrained by their location or by the nature of the trade they serve. Others are restricted by their charter of operation. Nevertheless, port involvement in physical distribution has enormous potential in terms of attracting cargo-related economic activities and providing a competitive edge.

In order to succeed in the new role they are taking on with regard to transportation and logistics, ports must also adapt themselves to the requirements of the new information and communications era. To integrate fully in the intermodal concept, seaports — like every other element in the transport system — must be equipped with information systems and have access to data bases. It is most unlikely to conceive of the efficient, fast handling of cargo throughout all links of the total transport chain without a computerized comprehensive information system. Compiling such a system is an issue that is high on the agenda of almost every leading container port.

On the other hand, the relative importance of some traditional port functions has suffered in the role-changing process. Traditionally, the chain of ocean transport trade was interrupted at the port itself. Inbound and outbound cargo were stored in warehouses at the port before they were loaded or after they had been discharged from ships. Containers, though, rapidly passed through the ports; moreover, the containers themselves provided a temporary commodity storage. Except, then, for the container freight station where cargo is consolidated, the need for port warehousing has been reduced. The trend is to relocate large warehouses, and the storage function itself, away from the ports. This decentralisation, which actually started with the relocation of commercial, manufacturing, and industrial activities to the fringes of the urban areas, has intensified. Many of the large warehouses adjacent to the piers that served the conventional general cargo system have consequently become obsolete. The attendant need for many conventional cargo-related services at the port — cooperage, bagging, weighing, measuring, inspecting, etc. — has in the process also been reduced.

PORT COMPETITION

Containerization, particularly in its intermodal stage, has altered the conventional marketing structure and hinterland relations of ports, and introduced new dimensions to port competition. In the pre-container era, ports basically competed on an intra-regional level. Each port carved out for itself a fairly well-defined hinterland, consisting mainly of the contiguous region. The port of New York competed principally with Baltimore and Boston, just as Hampton Roads vied with Savannah, Rotterdam with Antwerp, and Marseilles with Genoa. Inland transportation was unhelpful in breaking out of such confines as it could not then cope economically and efficiently with large cargo volumes over long-distance routes. Furthermore, the conventional liner operator abetted this "stability" by not being inclined to move from accepted ports, particularly if the commodity shippers were accustomed to specific routeings and had made warehousing and other arrangements accordingly.

The traditional constraints began to disappear with the intermodal phase. The entire trip from origin to final destination became the responsibility of one carrier, whose responsibility it was to design the entire route, including transfer points, according to a total distribution strategy. Shippers now had reason to be roused from their inertia. If the proposed integrated transport route presented to them by the responsible carrier was more attractive from both a time and cost point of view, why should they continue to be interested in a specific port? Particularly in the United States, the freedom and flexibility of shipping lines to develop a variety of efficient "door-to-door" routes, some of which by-passed traditional ports of call associated with a specific trade route, increased with deregulation.

Port competition, in consequence, shifted to the inter-regional level. The new port hinterlands are vast; indeed, they may encompass countries and even continents. For all practical purposes, the United States may be considered a single hinterland for any large US container port, just as all of Western and Central Europe may be viewed as a vast and common tributary area for ports so distantly spaced as Hamburg, Rotterdam, Antwerp, Le Havre, Marseilles and Trieste. In the expanded competitive arena, ironically, a neighbouring port may not be the most serious rival. With the economic, efficient inland transportation systems and with the development of through-rate practices and dynamic and geographically complex inland-distribution schemes such as minibridges, the port is now simply another link in the chain, a point smoothly passed on the way to a final destination.[4] The accessibility of a port to such inland transport systems, not only the quality of the port services themselves is a prime factor in the competition.

The new organizational structure of the traffic flow under the intermodal concept, in which the entire voyage from origin to final destination is covered under one bill of lading and a single rate, has made it very difficult for ports to evaluate their competitive position. The single rate quoted to the shipper by

4. Hayuth, Y. (1985), "Intermodalism and the US Port System", *Lloyd's Shipping Economist* 7, 4, pp. 18–20.

the agency or company controlling the cargo is based on a combination of costs related to each of the transport modes on the route. This does not necessarily imply, though, that the total cost is a summation of the lowest costs of each transport segment. A shipping company may select a port of call, not on the merit that it provides cheaper services, but on the basis of a comprehensive analysis of the total route. It may, in fact, choose to call at a more costly port because the advantages of inland transport or ocean routes from/to this port overcome the additional port costs. Thus, the conventional basis of competition among ports, improved efficiency and lower rates, may be insufficient or partly irrelevant; unfortunately for many ports, it is difficult, under the intermodal concept, to know how they have been priced by shipping lines or railroads compared to their competitors.

Thus, the basic criteria by which the selection of ports is made by shippers or transport companies have been modified. The relative importance of several traditional criteria has been reduced; other factors, and their components, have been altered, and new criteria have emerged.

It is more and more evident that competition among ports is being decided on the quality of their external relations. Obviously, the high daily operating cost of vessels and the large investments by railroads in rolling stock still make it imperative that a port serve its customers efficiently and at a competitive price. This ability, although an important consideration in the port selection process, is generally being viewed more as an obvious factor rather than a competitive edge. In the intermodal era, a port must be, and have, more in order to attract customers.

The accessibility of a port to the inland transport network has become a critical element in port competition. Railroads have always been important for the development of ports; however, the characteristics of the port-railway interrelationships are now the determining factors for ports competing in the intermodal arena. The quality of rail services that a port can offer can be evaluated from two points of view: first, the physical accessibility of the port to a railway system; second, the rates agreement and transport schemes that a port can manage to promote with the cooperation of a railway company. Traditionally, a port that had no access to a major railway system was seriously handicapped.

With intermodal transport, the issue has become more specific: the precise distance between the container terminal and the railhead is of utmost importance. As described in Chapter 3, European ports are better positioned in this regard than are most North American ports. Indeed, an effort to bring container terminal and railhead together is high on the agenda of most of the large ports in the United States. The joint project of the ports of Los Angeles and Long Beach, together with the Southern Pacific Transportation Company, to create a single intermodal container transfer facility nearer to the two ports is certainly a good example of the importance of easy accessibility — as well as of the changes in port competition criteria.

The location of a port near a navigable river was a major advantage particularly in regard to bulk commodities. The railways and the interstate highway systems generally transfer most of the general cargo commodities. Intermodal transportation has gradually returned the glory of inland waterways as an important transport mode for general cargo goods, this time in containers. The substantial volumes of containers moving by barges and the development of inland intermodal depots along the Rhine River evidence the success of ports, such as Rotterdam, in the intermodal competition.

If the spatial accessibility of ports to a railway network is a traditional factor in port competition that has taken on added meaning with intermodal transportation, the deep involvement of ports in lobbying, in pressuring for the cooperation of and for tariff agreements with railroads, and in assuming the initiator's role in promoting intermodal transport schemes is a new phenomenon. Since more ports than ever before are competing on the same, although extended, hinterland, it is obvious that a port that can present better accessibility to large inland transport networks, provide greater frequency of service, and offer lower rates will have an edge in the competition. These factors are so vital for ports competing in the intermodal era that it will even cause a port that is strictly competitive on the intra-regional level to cooperate and combine efforts with other ports in order to improve its position on the inter-regional level. The West German ports of Bremen, Bremerhaven, and Hamburg have joined forces to exert pressure on the central government to intervene in what they claim is unfair cross-border tariffs. Concerned at their slower rate of growth in container traffic compared to Belgian and Dutch ports, these three normally competing German ports have teamed up to argue that they are put at a competitive disadvantage *vis-à-vis* those other ports; the reason is the fixed rate system of the railways and intermodal road hauliers in Germany, compared to the less restricted rate structure prevailing in the Netherlands and Belgium. The efforts of the West German ports to attain greater flexibility in inland transport rates is to a great extent the result of the fast growth in container traffic on the River Rhine. The point, though, is that although these three ports compete against one another on one level, they found it advantageous to cooperate in an attempt to improve their position on another competitive level.

Other traditional competitive factors, such as the depth of the harbour and access channel or the availability of storage areas (including temporary storage), have gained significance because of the demand for larger cellular vessels with bigger draft and larger capacity. New factors, too, have entered the port competition equation. The command by a port of sophisticated information and communication systems and the availability of computerized cargo documentation and clearance systems are foremost among these factors.[5] If the through movement of cargo, coordination between transport modes, and the constant control of cargo comprise the essence of the intermodal transport concept, it is obvious that port customers are greatly concerned about the level of service they can obtain. Service includes not only the physical handling of the cargo, but also keeping track or tracing it en route and clearing it quickly and efficiently through the port.

The new competitive environment brought about by intermodality has raised yet another issue. In order to satisfy the demand of both transport carriers and commodity shippers, ports found they had to become more specialized. In the conventional port system, almost every port was equipped to handle a wide range of commodities and to provide almost all the required port services; this general role is not feasible for the intermodal port system. It is unlikely that all or even most ports would be able to provide all the services at a quality that port customers seek.

5. See also: Slack, B. (1985), "Containerization, Inter-port Competition and Port Selection", *Maritime Policy and Management* 12, 4, pp. 293–303.

How many ports can offer a large concentration of traffic and a high-volume, long-range inland transport corridor, for example? Moreover, it is not the intention of ship operators to call with their large, high-daily-operation-cost vessels at every port. Thus, the question arises: should ports ensure their future by complementing rather than competing with one another, at least on the inter-regional level?[6] A partial answer to this question is evident from two trends: restructuring the port-system hierarchy and load centre-feeder port interrelations.

LOAD CENTRES

The phenomenon of traffic concentration at a limited number of favoured seaports should not be evaluated as an outcome of the interport competitive struggle, but rather seen as a necessity in an industry, and in a total transport system, with limited capital and resources.

The centring of trade at selected ports did not start in the containerization era. Conventional break-bulk cargo liners spent a great deal of costly time in port, and the multiplication of ports and berths added to port-time and shifting expenses. For this reason, owners of deep-sea vessels were inclined to concentrate their services at fewer and fewer ports of call. By the early stages of containerization development in the United Kingdom, there was already a heavy concentration of deep-sea cargo liner sailings from Liverpool and London. Some 53% of United Kingdom exports to Asia and 64% of exports to Australia went through those two ports.[7]

Load centre implies a concentration of container traffic at a limited number of larger ports.[8] Other names, such as "pivot port"[9] and "assembly ports",[10] have been given to the phenomenon of traffic concentration at a few dominant container

6. Fleming, D. K. (1983), "Port Rivalry. Co-operation and Mergers", *Maritime Policy and Management*, 10, 3, pp. 207–210.

7. Port of London Authority, *Britain's Foreign Trade* (1965), London, p. 22.

8. Hayuth, Y. (1978), *Containerization and the Load Centre Concept*, Unpublished Ph.D dissertation (Seattle: University of Washington).

9. Bird, J. (1971), *Seaports and Seaport Terminals* (London: Hutchinson University Library).

10. The National Research Council (1976), *Port Development of the United States* (Washington, DC: National Academy of Sciences), p. 133.

ports. The principle of concentration of container traffic in a limited number of terminal areas has also been suggested by the European and international shipping communities. A. L. Latham-Koenig, in his evaluation of future trends and developments in the area of containerized transport in Europe, concluded: "There will be an inexorable trend toward fewer main ports of call for container ships and more feeder services."[11] An example cited was the pattern of calls of Sea-Land in Europe at that time (Bremerhaven, Grangemouth, Felixstowe, Rotterdam) as being indicative of the probable shape of the future concentration of containerized shipping. In a symposium at Bergen in 1973, E. Pollock of the British Transport Dock Board said that there was a limit to the number of ports that it would pay to link by direct services, not only because of ship size and cargo availability, but most importantly because of the turnaround time of ships in port.[12]

The rationale for so concentrating container traffic is best explained by examining the three principal segments of the integrated intermodal transportation system — the ocean voyage, the transit through the seaport, and the inland transport journey.

The high operating costs of a container vessel, up to $40,000 daily, and the costs of port visits induce containership owners to rationalize their operations by cutting down on port time. There are two fundamental time-reducing strategies: decreasing the turnaround time in port and reducing the number of ports of call. Multiple port visits, naturally, increase the carrier's operating costs, for at each port there are unavoidable charges for such services as towing, pilotage and dockage. Additional time needed for slow entrance to ports, manoeuvring in the harbour, and non-working hours by port personnel further diminish the annual revenue-earning performance of a vessel. A reduction in port time is particularly important for the larger, more expensive containerships. The attractive economies of scale achieved by large vessels serving longer routes therefore argue for the concentration of container traffic at a few commodious ports at each end of the trade route.

11. Latham-Koenig, A. L. (1970), "The Development of Container Transport in the Future of the European Ports", in *The Future of European Ports* (Bruge: College of Europe), p. 682.

12. Pollock, E. (1973), Report on International Symposium (Bremen: Shipping Research Institute).

From the port's viewpoint, the claim of economies of scale in port operations is not unfounded. Fast turn-around time by ships considerably increases the port's annual cargo throughput. A small number of terminals can handle a much larger volume, and can capture (and transship) a large share of the trade. As the scale of operations increases, the fixed cost spreads over more movement units, which thus reduces the cost of handling a unit of cargo.

The potential saving in inland transportation costs also induces the sea-going carrier to seek economies of scale by concentrating traffic in fewer ports, this time in order to penetrate the interior with high volume on a specific overland route. Indeed, the load centre concept calls for the development of high-priority trunk lines between load centre ports and major market centres. The load centres then can offer attractive rate schemes, speed, service regularity, and a high volume of inland traffic, all of which are mutual and interrelated objectives shared by carriers, shippers, and ports.

Container ports in the major containerized trades certainly form a concentrated system. In North America, the handling of containers is well established among all the deep-water general cargo ports (Figure 9). In 1985, total container traffic passing through US ports amounted to about 11.2 million TEU, of which 6.6 million TEU (59.3%) was handled by five major ports: New York/New Jersey, Seattle, Long Beach, Los Angeles, and Oakland. This concentration of activity is better illustrated by a regional analysis.

The North American East Coast container port system is clearly dominated by the bi-state Port of New York/New Jersey. In 1985, this port handled over 2.4 million TEU, three times as many containers as did Baltimore, the second largest container port on the East Coast. The premier position of the port of New York, though, is progressively and substantially being eroded, despite the absolute growth in container traffic. In 1970, New York handled 72 per cent of the containers that moved through the entire North American Atlantic Coast. By 1985, its share had been reduced to only 47 per cent. The competition came from neighbouring ports such as Boston, Philadelphia and Baltimore, but the port was also affected by the operation of cross-country container movements, which has diverted Far Eastern cargo from East Coast ports to the West Coast.

US West Coast ports have been in the front line of containerization since the early 1960s. They are also the most active and advanced ports in the development of intermodal transport systems in the United States. In 1985, these ports handled 4.4 million TEU, which represented about 40 per cent of the total US container traffic. Changes in international liner trading patterns, particularly the burgeoning importance of the United States-Far East trade, have obviously contributed significantly to the growth in West Coast container traffic. A shift in the centre of gravity of American liner trade from the Atlantic to the Pacific Ocean has occurred in the past decade. Not only has the share of Far Eastern and South East Asian trade with the United States risen, from 29.7 per cent in 1972 to 37.6 per cent in 1983, compared with an almost identical decline in the share of European trade with the United States, from 36.7 per cent to 29.1 per cent over the same period; the West Coast share of the Far East and South East Asian trade with the United States has gone up as well.[13] This growth in the volume of containerized trade in the Pacific Basin would not have had its full impact on US West Coast ports, however, without the development of intermodality, which fostered overland transcontinental container movements.

Unlike the East Coast port system, which as described is clearly dominated by one port, four West Coast ports — Seattle, Long Beach, Los Angeles, and Oakland — all stand in the forefront of the competition to become principal centres for intermodal shipment. These four load centres together handled in 1985 more than 4.2 million TEU, which represented about 84% of the entire container traffic on the US Continental Pacific Coast. Of these four, the port of Long Beach, with 1,444,000 TEU in 1985, was the main container port on the coast and, indeed, the second largest container port in North America. Having a much smaller local market and population base than its competitors to the south, the port of Seattle, the main Pacific north-west port, is greatly dependent on its intermodal role in order to maintain its status as a major import gateway for Far Eastern cargo destined for the Mid-West and the East Coast.

13. Port of Oakland (1984), *Liner Trade Analysis, Pacific Basin Countries*, (Oakland: Port Research Department).

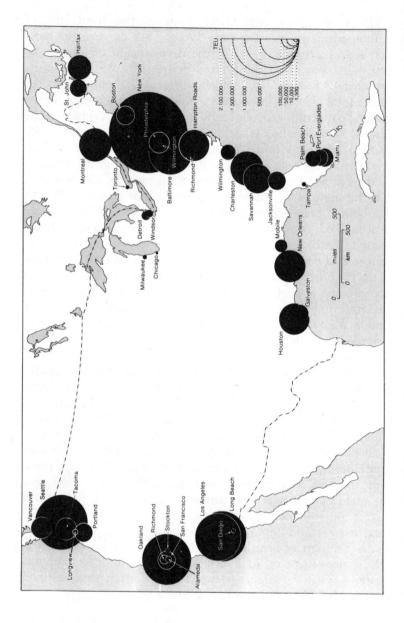

Figure 9. North American container port system, 1984

In Europe, container port traffic has been well established since the late 1960s. In 1985, European ports handled 14.4 million TEU (Figure 10).[14] Despite the fact that 87 European seaports that year handled more than 1000 TEU each, more than twice as many ports as in North America, the concentration characteristics of the "new world" repeat themselves in the "old". The port of Rotterdam, the largest container port in the world, handled more than 2.6 million TEU in 1985, or about 18% of the entire European container traffic (including the UK). Europe's five largest container ports — Rotterdam, Antwerp, Hamburg, Bremen and Felixstowe — handled about 48.6% of the total European container traffic that year. The four largest ports of north-west Europe were responsible for 94.7% of the container traffic of the entire region.

The Far East presents an advanced container port system, but here too, container traffic is concentrated in a limited number of ports. As a matter of fact, six of the ten largest container ports in the world in 1985 were located in the Far East. In South East Asia, which transferred about 54% of all Far East containers in 1985, 80 per cent of this traffic was handled by four ports: Hong Kong, Singapore, Kaohsiung, and Keelung.

The concept of a load centre goes back to the beginnings of containerization; however, the reality of regional load centre ports is being fed by the growth of intermodalism.[15] Several factors can explain the renewed discussion of the potential of the load centre. For one, the introduction of jumbo container vessels by US Lines, the large vessels employed by Evergreen Lines on its round-the-world service, and the bigger than Panamax-size vessels built for American President Lines in 1986 renewed the pressure on ship operators to rationalize their port schedules and to select a limited number of ports of call. For another, the role of the railroads, always a key factor for the development of load centres, magnified with the new double-stack container trains. A third factor was the deregulation of the transport industry in the United States, and the US Shipping Act of 1984, which better enabled

14. The figures include the Scandinavian ports. Without these ports, the figure is 13.8 million TEU.

15. This idea was supported in the presentations of A. Tozzoli, director of port department of the Port of New York/New Jersey, and J. Majunckin, executive director of the Port of Long Beach, at the Fall Meeting of the Containerization and Intermodal Institute, 1985.

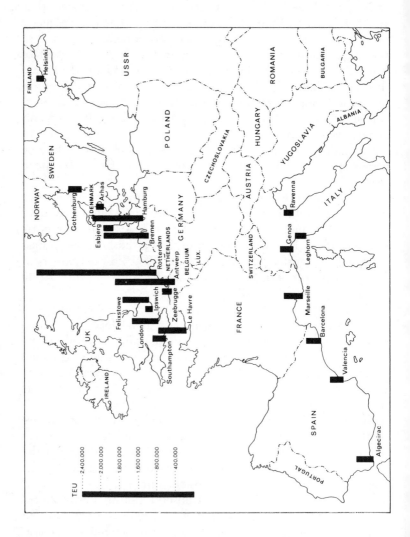

Figure 10. European container port system, 1984

shipping lines to offer point-to-point rates, and thus to enhance their flexibility in selecting ports of call.

In the light of improved potential for the load centre concept with intermodality, at least in theory, it is essential to examine the trend, over time, by port systems to concentrate activities. To obtain a picture of the changes in the degree of concentration in the structure of the United States and European port systems, the Lorenz Curve and the Gini Coefficient were employed. The Lorenz Curve measures the cumulative percentage of port size, as indicated by the volume of containers (TEU) of each port, against the cumulative percentage of the number of container ports in each region. The Gini Coefficient represents the ratio of the area of concentration to the total area below the equal distribution diagonal and bounded by the axis of the diagram.[16]

The results demonstrate a constant trend towards growing concentration in all three regions, each region at its own pace. The degree of actual change, however, is relatively moderate compared with the expected potential change to more concentrated systems. The larger container vessels that have entered service over the years, the increased traffic through intermodal transport schemes like minibridge (see Chapter 6), and the deregulation of the United States transport industry since 1980 did not yield corresponding development towards a more concentrated port system. Moreover, analysis (with the Gini Coefficient) of the container traffic results in North America between 1970–1985 shows that the North America container port system has actually become a less concentrated system.

Two main reasons may account for the fact that despite the theoretical, operational and economic rationales behind the load centre concept, ports systems, particularly in North America, did not move towards a more concentrated system — and may even be displaying a reverse trend.

Containerization, like many other technological innovations, concentrated in its early stages on a very small number of centres where it had established itself. In later stages of the innovation life cycle, during the diffusion process, some of the initial advantages of the innovation faded, and increased challenge arose from the periphery. On the one hand, the larger ports are faced

16. For more details, see: Needham, D. (1969), *Economic Analysis and Industrial Structure* (New York: Holt, Rinehart and Winston).

with increasing expansion difficulties either because of a lack of available space (e.g., the Port of Seattle) or because of environmental constraints (e.g., California ports). On the other hand, the smaller ports, under the threat of losing still more cargo to their larger, better equipped competitors, are faced with local political and economic pressures, forcing them to yield up attractive terms for shipping lines in a desperate attempt to increase container traffic. Developments in US Southern Atlantic ports, in the Port of San Francisco, and in the Port of Galveston, provide examples of this situation.

Another fact that helps to explain the trend to a less concentrated port system has to do with the very operation of the load centre concept. Shipping lines that call only at a limited number of ports have several advantages, as previously discussed; however, this does not necessarily imply that all shipping lines will choose the same ports as their load centres. For its around-the-world service, United States Lines selected the port of Savannah as its load centre in the South Atlantic, while Evergreen Lines preferred the neighbouring port of Charleston. Delta Line decided to concentrate its transshipment activities in Philadelphia instead of its previous centre, New York. Selection by major carriers of different ports for their load centre operations contributes to a more equally distributed container port system. The concentration, though, seems to manifest itself more at the level of the shipping companies than at the port system level.

Although the claim has generally been made that existing load centre ports benefit from the development of intermodal transport, the actuality may prove to be the other way around. Intermodality may open — in fact, it already has — new hopes for smaller ports. These ports, and the latecomers that have not yet fully committed themselves financially and spatially to one method or another of containerization, may be in a better position to adapt their facilities to the new requirements of true intermodal movement. The ability of the port of Tacoma to meet the in-terminal railhead needs of Sea-Land better than Seattle provides the best illustration of this new reality so far.

CHAPTER 6

Inland transport and landbridges

Containerization has greatly improved the efficiency of both ocean transportation and port operations. The advantages and contribution of these improvements, however, might have been jeopardized without a parallel development in inland transportation.

The commodity shipper and the goods receiver have always been concerned with total distribution costs. These costs, in overseas trade, generally have three major components — inland transportation, port transit, and ocean voyage. In the pre-container era, the ocean carrier's primary concern and responsibility were, in most cases, confined to cargo loading, vessel steaming, and cargo discharging. With the advent and advancement of containerization and intermodality, shipping lines had to stretch both their functional and spatial operations beyond their conventional role in the freight transport system. Ocean carriers had to acquire a door-to-door, rather than a port-to-port, perspective, and they soon joined the commodity shipper in a concern for total distribution costs and total transit time. They were, in a word, increasingly concerned not only with the transport service performed by the containership, but also with the quality and costs involved in overland transport, which was of necessity linked to door-to-door service. Without doubt, this implied an increase in the relative importance to liner operators of inland transport modes, such as railways and trucks and also ports.

Containerization and the improvements in inland transport networks had, for ocean carriers, perhaps the untoward effect of bettering the competitive position of inland carriers. The development of national highway systems, particularly in the United States and Europe, the adaptation of long-distance truck haulage to the container system, the introduction of container unit trains and the double-stack container rail cars have all acted to lower the unit costs of overland transportation. This, in turn, encouraged the development of inland distribution in which overland movements (of railroads and trucks) could compete successfully with the high-daily-operating-cost container vessels on short as well as on long-distance routes. This chapter focuses on two such concepts, closely related, that were greatly affected by containerization and intermodality — the hinterland and the landbridge.

THE HINTERLAND CONCEPT

Hinterland has been defined as "organized and developed land space which is connected with a port by means of transport lines, and which receives or ships goods through that port".[1] Although precise definitions may vary, a hinterland is generally considered a tributary area, the "backyard" of a port, and a functional region in which different internal points are linked to a port.[2] Many studies have attempted to delineate a hinterland for a specific port; however, the single line on the map, the boundary, and the bounded area are gross generalizations hiding many anomalies. Although the treatment of a hinterland as an area predominantly under the influence of one port may have some merit, it is risky in an era of rapid change to view the port hinterland as a static concept.

In the competitive fray, a port hinterland today expands or contracts, sometimes very quickly. Changes in hinterland dimensions also occur from natural causes, such as winter icing of ports, or as a result of political events. Exogenous economic factors may prove a shaping factor; where centralized governments control port operations, for instance, government policy favouring one port over another can affect the size of a port hinterland.

The examples cited illustrate changes which will affect certain ports at certain times but which will not have a general or world-wide impact. Intermodal transportation, on the other hand, has extensively modified the basic hinterland patterns established by conventional break-bulk cargo — and on a global scale.[3]

1. Weigend, G. G. (1958), "Some Elements in the Study of Port Geography", *Geographical Review* 48, pp. 185–200.

2. Bird, J. (1971), *Seaports and Seaport Terminals* (London: Hutchinson University Library).

3. Hayuth, Y. (1982), "Intermodal Transportation and the Hinterland Concept", *Tijdschrift Voor Economische en Sociale Geografie* 73, pp. 13–21.

The traditional hinterland concept tends to assign to each port a fairly well-defined tributary area for most cargo movements through the port, usually consisting of the port city and the contiguous region. One important factor limiting the size of the hinterland in the conventional general cargo system was the greater expense of land transportation compared to sea transport, which led ships customarily to call at a series of neighbouring ports. The conventional liner operator, furthermore, was not inclined to move from accepted ports, especially if the commodity shippers were accustomed to specific routings and made warehousing and other arrangements accordingly. Inertia has certain short-term cost advantages.

With the development of containerization and, particularly, intermodal transportation systems, many of the traditional constraints began to disappear. For one thing, the entire voyage, now a "door-to-door" service, tended to become the responsibility of a single carrier in the new inland distribution strategy. Thus, may shippers are no longer interested in a specific port or its temporary storage and handling capabilities. The carrier relieves them of this concern. The port is simply a point, smoothly passed, on the way to a final destination.

Intermodal transportation added to the state of flux of hinterland delineation by increasing not only the potential extent of the hinterland but also the dimensions of its geographical diversions. Today, inland points are linked with and trade via several ports. The shipper and receiver at any location have at their disposal a large variety of effective options and alternative routes and ports. Trade lines connecting inland points with ports frequently intersect one another, and conventional hinterlands now generally overlap. The tributary areas of ports can be vastly extended to stretch over entire countries or continents. By the same token, a continent may serve as a common hinterland for ports located thousands of miles apart. If a port's trade promotion offices indicate potential hinterlands, then the fact that ports so distantly spaced as Charleston, Seattle, Houston, and Savannah, for example, maintain trade offices in Chicago suggests the complexity of modern hinterland delineation.

The inland distribution of cargo is dynamic and geographically complex. There is less reason than ever before to treat hinterlands as areas with distinct boundaries. It has been the carrier more than the shipper that has been behind these changes. Ocean liners, together with railways and trucking firms, have developed integrated transport systems that have transformed the traditional hinterland concept out of all recognition.

THE LANDBRIDGE PHENOMENON

The development of landbridges is perhaps one of the most significant manifestations of these newly developed, integrated systems. The general concept of "landbridge" signifies the utilization of land transport for a part of what would normally be entirely an ocean voyage. The purposes of transport by landbridge are saving in transportation costs and reduction in total transit time. The potential saving in inland transportation costs induces ocean carriers to seek economies of scale in inland movements by concentrating traffic at a limited number of ports having superior access to major inland transportation corridors. In this way, the carriers can penetrate the interior with high volume on a specified overland route.

Long-haul overland routes competing with traditional ocean transport movements are not restricted only to one region of the world or to a specific trade route. The Canadian landbridge, for example, has been operating since the mid-1960s, and seaborne containers started to move across the United States in the early 1970s. Landbridges are not, of course, limited to North America, as witness the Trans-Siberian landbridge and the ones across Mexico and in the Middle East.

One may assume that the landbridge concept is a new phenomenon resulting from the advancement of containerization and intermodal transportation. There is a claim, however, that the idea of the United States as a landbridge is as old as the first transcontinental railroad in the second half of the nineteenth century. Japan-New York trade before the opening of the Panama Canal mainly used the route of the transpacific and the transcontinental railway rather than the ocean route via Suez. In another part of the world, the ancient caravan trails between Asia and Europe, e.g., the "silk trail", were for hundreds of years important trading routes and communication links between widely divergent cultures. With improved shipping techniques, maritime transportation replaced these overland routes. Ironically, perhaps, modern improvements in ocean transportation and the development of intermodality revived the long-forgotten "silk trail". It has now become a busy trading route serving the flourishing trade between the Far East and Europe, but is today known as the Trans-Siberian Landbridge.

NORTH AMERICAN LANDBRIDGES

More than one landbridge operates across North America (Figure 11). In the United States, first Seatrain in January 1972 and later US Lines initiated through transport of containers between Japan and Europe across the United States in cooperation with five railways, particularly the Sante Fe, in effect forming a transcontinental railway system. The Canadian landbridge had actually started a few years earlier, respectively linking transatlantic and transpacific ocean carriers with rail piggyback from East Coast ports, particularly Halifax and Saint John, and Vancouver on the West Coast. The importance of these North American landbridges was not in the volume of traffic they managed to attract, which was always small, but their pioneering role in intermodal transport. With both landbridges, the entire voyage was controlled and under the responsibility of one transport mode — ocean shipping — which made the decisions about the routeing and selection of ports of call. Another distinguishing characteristic was that the entire voyage from Europe to the Far East or vice-versa was covered by a single bill of lading issued by the shipping line or an NVOCC.

South of the United States, a Mexican landbridge — an idea that goes back to 1850 — was started up in the late 1970s. This 180-mile "bridge" offers both railway and highway services between the port of Coatzacoalos on the Gulf of Mexico and the port of Salina Cruz on the Pacific Coast. The Mexican landbridge saves about 1,000 miles on a trip from New York to Los Angeles, compared to the route via the Panama canal. The Mexican landbridge, however, despite the encouragement of and investments made by the Mexican government, has failed to attract much business from its competitors, the various forms of landbridges in the United States and Canada to the north and the Panama Canal to the south.

A far more vital trade route, one with significant volumes of containerized traffic, is the United States minibridge. A somewhat different concept, minibridge denotes "the movement of containers under a single ocean bill of lading from one country via a vessel to a port in another country, thence by rail minibridge to a second port city, terminating at the rail carrier's terminal".[4] Minibridge tariffs are published by the shipping lines, which negotiate the rates of the other transport modes that have a share in the intermodal journey. Under this concept, Asian cargo, for example, may be transported across the Pacific by sea-going vessel and then hauled overland from a US West Coast port to a final destination at one of the ports along the East Coast. Minibridge services may involve less than continent-wide movements. European cargo, for example, may be transported overland from an East Coast port like Charleston and then to New Orleans by rail. The minibridge differs from the landbridge in that the former does not involve sea-land-sea movements of cargo, only sea-land transport (Figure 12).

Minibridge service was first offered in late 1971, when transatlantic cargo destined for a United States Gulf port was off-loaded at an East Coast port. Since then, this type of traffic has grown considerably, but particularly in the early 1980s (Table 3). By the mid-1980s, minibridges had become a major competitor of the all-water Panama Canal route. Its penetration of the East Coast market is significant. In 1983, the eastbound minibridge via West Coast ports captured nearly 30 per cent of the liner trade that would have gone to Atlantic and Gulf Coasts via the Panama Canal. This figure is double the 14.8 per cent in 1976 (Figure 13). Minibridge traffic, however, represents a very imbalanced trade. Far East liner cargo destined for the East and Gulf Coast regions and moving via West Coast ports, i.e., minibridge traffic — totalled over 1.7 million short tons in 1983 and accounted for 24 per cent of all liner imports off loaded on the West Coast. This volume was far larger than that sent in the opposite direction.

4. *Containerization International Yearbook*, 1977.

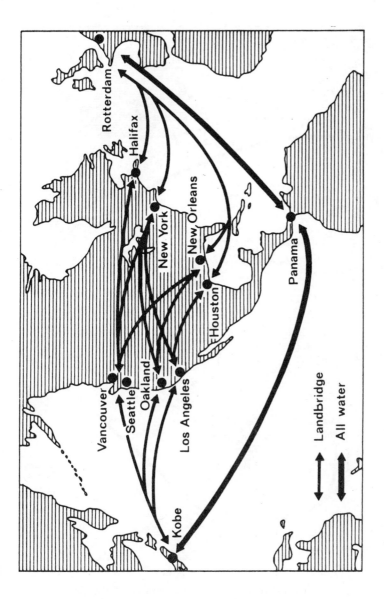

Figure 11. The North American Landbridge

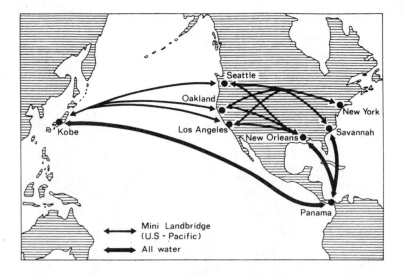

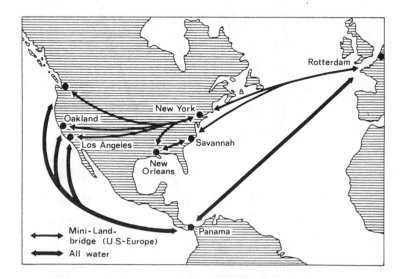

Figure 12. The mini-landbridge transport routes

Source: Hayuth, Y., *Tijdschrift Voor Econ. en Soc. Geografie*, 73 (1982), pp. 13–21

Table 3. United States minibridge traffic, 1978 – 1983 (thousands of short tons)

A. *Asian minibridge imports to the United States*

East Coast customs district — destinations	West Coast customs district — unloading					
	1978	1979	1980	1981	1982	1983
North Atlantic region	597.5	544.6	656.1	717.2	778.7	960.2
South Atlantic region	87.9	102.0	113.4	121.2	138.5	174.4
Gulf Coast region	477.2	433.1	480.8	624.1	592.4	610.2
Total	1,162.6	1,079.7	1,250.3	1,462.5	1,509.6	1,744.8

B. *European minibridge imports to the United States*

East Coast customs district — unloading	West Coast customs district — destinations					
	1978	1979	1980	1981	1982	1983
North Atlantic region	45.5	47.5	48.5	44.0	44.9	44.3
South Atlantic region	45.7	39.1	16.8	10.0	18.2	35.3
Gulf region	75.0	113.9	106.2	113.1	128.5	158.2
Total	166.2	200.5	169.5	167.1	191.6	237.8

Source: US Bureau of Census, foreign trade tapes SM 304; and Port of Oakland, *Liner Trade Analysis*, 1984

The development of minibridge traffic was initially enhanced by the standardization of container units; later, it was given a boost by the advancement of intermodal transport, particularly the much improved rail services. The minibridge has a substantial effect on traditional port hinterlands and, of course, on transport itineraries. For instance, aluminium coils produced in the State of Washington could quite easily be routed overseas via the nearby port of Seattle. Instead, the containerized coils have been transported by rail to Houston, Texas, on the Gulf, then forwarded by ship to consignees in Rotterdam — and in a shorter time. Minibridge, as this example shows, has a potential for shifts in the trade flow from one seaboard to another.

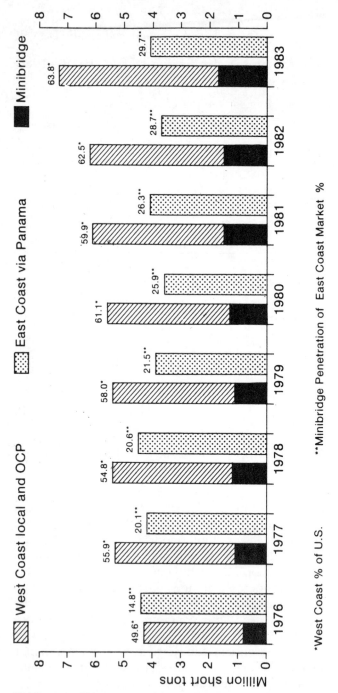

Figure 13. US imports from Asia, by coastal destinations and transport modes

Source: Port of Oakland, *Trade Analysis — Pacific Basin*, 1984

From the shipper's viewpoint, the major advantage of the minibridge is the wider range of services offered. The shipper has a greater choice of transport modes and vessel schedules. There is no longer any need to depend on one or two nearby ports when the services of many more ports are available. This, of course, creates a more complex hinterland picture, with interior points "shared" by an increasing number of ports.

From the shipping line's standpoint, minibridge provides an opportunity to streamline operations. The ship operator cannot be made to call at a given port, regardless of the port facilities, just to serve certain customers. The ocean carrier is now able to select ports which have the appropriate accommodations, which fit the itinerary, and which will still enable serving the same customers. Finally, the minibridge concept accentuates the tendency of transatlantic and transpacific traffic to concentrate at a few ports, with obviously larger hinterlands, thus helping the carrier to achieve better utilization of ships and more efficient inland movements of containers.

Although the vast majority of ocean carriers operating in the transpacific trade still serve the United States East Coast with all-water modes, a significant shift to minibridge services can be observed. The gradual increase in Panama'nian control of the canal, expectation of higher canal charges, and the limitation of the dimensions of the canal's locks *vis-à-vis* future container vessels are important factors responsible for this shift. Any further increase in vessel dimensions above those of US Line's jumbo 4,482 TEU-capacity Econship, which entered service in late 1984, would prevent such containerships from using the canal. American President Lines have already placed an order for larger than "Panamax" size container vessels.

The greatest shortcoming of all-water operations through the Panama Canal, however, has to do with distance and transit time. The route from Japan to New York via the Pacific North-West and minibridge service is about 5,000 kilometres shorter than the route via the Panama Canal; it is also 7–10 days faster. In 1986, US Lines was offering a 24-day, all-water service between the Far East and US East Coast, compared with the 14–18-day transit operated by APL. Several shipping companies, led by APL, have argued that for high-value cargo and the practice then recently adopted by businesses and industries of maintaining lower levels of inventories, the time-saving factor will drive more cargo to the intermodal system.

"Microbridge" is yet another form of intermodal system operating in the United States. The microbridge is a through container service to and from interior points in the United States and involving at least two modes of transportation, generally ocean and rail. The concept is also known as IPI (Interior Point Intermodal). Microbridge differs from minibridge by avoiding double port transfers within the transcontinental trip. Under microbridge services, which are used by many shipping lines, containers may be transferred from any interior location in the United States to either of the coasts on the way to a final destination across the ocean. The entire service is covered by a single rate and a single bill of lading issued by a steamship line or by an NVOCC. As with the landbridge and minibridge concepts, neither the shipper nor the receiver has any impact on the routeing and port selection used by the microbridge service.

TRANS-SIBERIAN LANDBRIDGE

The old transport route connecting the Far East and Europe overland has been revived in the intermodal era. In April 1907, Osaka Shosen Kaisha, a Japanese steamship line, opened the Vladivostok trade route for carrying cargo and passengers to Europe via the Siberian railway. The first containers traversed the Siberian Landbridge in 1967. Only in 1971, though, did this landbridge become an accepted container route.

The Trans-Siberian Landbridge consists of four different intermodal systems that operate on both westbound and eastbound routes (Figure 14).

THE OCEAN-RAIL ROUTE

Cargo is transported by containership from a range of Japanese ports to the two eastern Soviet ports of Nakhodka and Vostochny. Then the containers are carried by the Siberian railway in a dedicated, 110 TEU train through main centres, like Moscow and Chelyabinsk, to the principal USSR border transfer points, such as Chop in Czechoslovakia, Brest in Poland, Djulfa in Iran, Kushka in Afghanistan, Ungeny in Romania, and Luzakia in Finland. Finally, the containers are hauled by train, on a different gauge, to multiple destinations in Eastern and Western Europe, Scandinavia, and the Middle East. Transit time for this very long route, over 13,000 kilometres for some destinations, is from 25–35 days.

THE OCEAN-RAIL-OCEAN ROUTE

This route takes cargo from Yokohama, Kobe, or other ports in Japan on board a Japanese or Russian steamship liner to Nakhodka or Vostochny, then by train to ports on the Baltic or the Black Sea, like Leningrad, Riga, Tallin, or Ilyichevsk, and again by ocean transportation to destinations in the Mediterranean area, Western Europe, or Scandinavia. Transit time on this particular intermodal route is between 30 and 40 days.

THE OCEAN-RAIL-TRUCK ROUTE

This triple transport-mode route connects Japan with Central and Western Europe as follows: container vessel from Japan to the eastern Soviet ports, the Siberian railway to Moscow, and on to transfer points at Vysoko-Litovsk, from there by truck to final destinations in West Germany, France, or Switzerland.

THE OCEAN-TRUCK-AIR-TRUCK ROUTE

Involving a four-fold transfer, this is the newest intermodal option of the Trans-Siberian Landbridge. Organised by the British Euro Container Transport Inc. in 1983, the service employs ocean carriage from Japan to the port of Nakhodka, and then truck haulage to Vladivostock, where the cargo is loaded on an Aeroflot jet that flies to Luxembourg, from which it is moved, generally by truck, to final destinations in Western Europe. Guaranteed door-to-door service on this route is 15 days.

Since 1972 Siberian landbridge container traffic, strongly

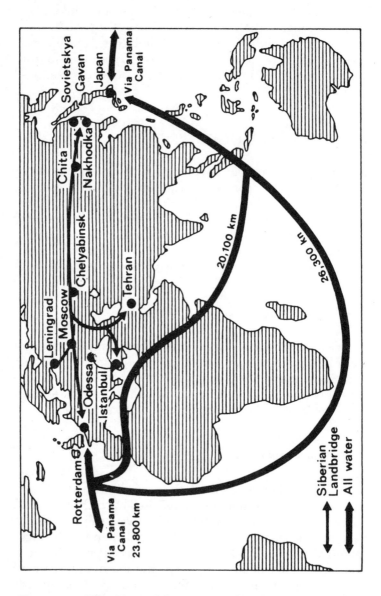

Figure 14. The Trans-Siberian Landbridge transport route
Source: Hayuth, Y., *Tidschrift Voor Econ. en Soc. Geografie*, 73 (1982), pp. 13–21

promoted by the Soviet Union, has increased rapidly, reaching a 90–100,000 TEU annual level by the mid-1980s. More than 1,000,000 TEU have been transferred via the bridge since the early 1970s. With such a volume of traffic, the Trans-Siberian Landbridge is a serious competitor of the all-water services between the Far East and Europe. The potential of this bridge traffic, furthermore, has been enhanced by the growing trend of the Soviet fleet to act as a cross trader in many routes, thus "channelling" container traffic from Australia and South-East Asian points towards the bridge. It is estimated that about 20 per cent of the total container trade between Japan and Europe was using the Siberian route in the mid-1980s. Indeed, this caused great concern to the ocean carriers in this trade, producing complaints of unfair pricing practices by the Soviets and the undercutting of maritime-conference rates by up to 25 per cent.

The Trans-Siberian Landbridge is several thousand miles shorter than any alternative route from the Far East to Western Europe. Its great advantage in distance, however, has not been translated into a saving in time. Before the fuel crisis in the late 1970s, ships could sail this route via the Suez Canal in 21 days; the Trans-Siberian Railroad needed 45 days. With the introduction of fuel economies and reduced vessel speeds, the ocean voyage increased to about 28 days. The land route has improved but still needs about 35 days.

In addition to its lower rates, the Trans-Siberian Landbridge offers other advantages: better accessibility to inland locations in Europe, an alternative route to the Middle East, and the avoidance of heavily congested Middle East ports — particularly true in the late 1970s but still a valid advantage nearly a decade later while the prolonged Iran-Iraq war prevented safe access to many of the region's seaports. (The war, though, has had an adverse influence on the purchasing power of the countries involved, and the large drop in Iranian imports from Japan hit the Siberian Landbridge traffic hard, particularly in 1985.)

The problems of the Trans-Siberian Landbridge are not at all marginal. Throughout the 1970s and the first half of the 1980s, many shippers were not attracted by intermodal bridge services, despite some of its advantages (reduced freight rates, to name just one). The unreliability inherent in transporting containers in a long and complex system, with little information on the cargo obtainable while en route, has been a great obstacle to the development of the traffic. The extremely unbalanced trade (most of the trade is westbound), the harsh Siberian winters, and claims of inefficient handling of containers at the transfer points are also among the problems of this trade route.

The Soviets, being aware that the quality of service is the major constraint on this service, are continuously introducing improvements; among them regular and express unit trains, a second parallel rail line at the western end of Siberia between Baikal and Amur, and a computerized tracing system of the containers "en route". The aim of all these improvements has been to upgrade the competitive position of the intermodal Siberian route *vis-à-vis* the all-water marine conferences.

The Trans-Siberian Landbridge illustrates the considerable change that has taken place in the traditional hinterland patterns of general cargo trade. One need only compare the movement of containers today from Europe to the Far East, via Siberia, to the delineation of the hinterlands of Rotterdam, Hamburg, and Bremen in the first half of this century as described in two studies that appeared in 1951.[5] In both studies, these hinterlands were seen not to penetrate deeper than the western edges of Eastern Europe.

Finally, the separation of the foreland-hinterland relationship (and delineations) of a port into two labelled packages represents a false dichotomy.[6] Both the North American landbridges and the Trans-Siberian Landbridge illustrate the fact that the so-called foreland and hinterland of many ports can now be treated as one.

LANDBRIDGES IN THE MIDDLE EAST

Intermodal landbridges in the Middle East were initiated as a result of political events in the region. The closure of the Suez Canal to shipping in 1967 brought about the need to search for a viable alternative to the regular trade routes. The canal closure particularly affected the Gulf States, for which the Cape route

5. Morgan, F. W. (1948), "The Pre-War Hinterlands of the German North Sea Ports", *Transactions of the Institute of British Geographers* 14, pp. 47–55.
6. Robinson, R. (1970), "The Hinterland-Foreland Continuum: Concept and Methodology", *Professional Geographer* 12, pp. 307–310.

was an extensive diversion so far as their trade with Europe was concerned. The need for alternative routes became critical with the increase in fuel prices, which brought in enormous revenues for the oil-rich countries in the Gulf peninsula. The petrol dollars, in turn, engendered a wave of import goods to these countries; however, this sudden demand for shipping met with an almost obsolete supply of port facilities. The unavoidable result was record congestion and waiting times for vessels in the Gulf ports in the late 1970s, which was yet another good reason to search for an alternative overland intermodal service.

The Turkish landbridge was created to solve these problems. European cargo bound for major places in the Gulf, such as Baghdad, Basrah, Tehran, Tabriz, Kuwait, Riyadh, and Bahrain, was transported (mainly) by sea to the Turkish Mediterranean ports of Mersin and Iskenderun and then hauled by truck across Turkey to the Gulf region. All-truck services from Europe to the Middle East were also available.

The viability of the Turkish landbridge was tested when the Suez Canal route was reopened for navigation at the end of 1976, and vast investments in port facilities led to Gulf ports having among the most modern container terminals in the world. Despite many predictions to the contrary, the Turkish landbridge did not cease operation. Several reasons may explain the survival power of this intermodal route. Inertia, commitments, and investments in the landbridge have probably had a short-term effect. The attractiveness of this landbridge service in terms of cost and transit time, compared to the much longer all-water route via Suez, Bab-el-Mandel, and the Straits of Hormuz, is also an important factor. No doubt, too, the war between Iran and Iraq and the inability of ports in these two countries to offer safe, efficient services have helped keep the Turkish landbridge in operation. Although exact statistics on the volume of this traffic are not available, almost all the landbridge services offered in the mid-1980s by more than ten steamship lines were directed to destinations in Iran and Iraq. On the other hand, the vast improvements in port and shipping services in the rest of the Gulf countries reduced the role of this landbridge in their trade. The ports of Mersin and Iskenderun continue to be the two main gateways and transfer points from ocean to land transportation on the Turkish landbridge.

Another intermodal landbridge formed against the background

of the closure of the Suez Canal is the Kedem Landbridge, also known as the Negev Continental Bridge (NCB). The Kedem Landbridge was designed to transfer containerized shipments between Europe and the Mediterranean, at one end, and the Indian Ocean and Far East, at the other end. Like the Turkish landbridge, the Kedem Landbridge offered an alternative route to the blocked Suez Canal and did not cease operations with the reopening of the canal.

The NCB runs between the Israeli port of Ashdod on the Mediterranean coast and the port of Eilat on the Red Sea, a distance of about 300 kilometres; it is officially operated by the Kedem Landbridge Company, a subsidiary of the Zim Navigation Company.[7] This landbridge is, in fact, part of a world-wide intermodal transport system operated by Zim, one link in a complex chain. Zim Container Services operates a global network, with one trading line, originating at the Port of Haifa, serving the Mediterranean, USA (East and West Coasts), Japan, and Hong Kong; and a second line, originating at the Red Sea port of Eilat, serving East Africa, India, Australia, and the Far East. The viability of the NCB and its role in the total system are explained by three principal factors.

First, Kedem company containers mostly use vacant or under-utilized space on Zim container ships calling at Israel's Mediterranean and Red Sea ports. The containers moved by this landbridge service, therefore, incur only the marginal operating costs of transport on both main legs of the multi-modal journey. In addition, the Israel Ports Authority offers reduced port tariffs to landbridge traffic that would not otherwise pass through Israeli ports.

Second, the landbridge helps to correct traffic imbalances on various Zim trade routes. By offering a reduced rate for cargo on a return transport leg on ships that would otherwise carry only empty containers, the shipping company can reduce the economic penalties resulting from trade imbalances. Such imbalances may be long-term, reflecting the nature of the trade, or they may result from a sudden surge of trade on one leg of a journey.

Third, the landbridge can be economically viable within the wider system if a cargo that has to move from an origin to a

7. Stern, E., Hayuth, Y., and Gradus, Y. (1983), "The Negev Continental Bridge: A Chain in an Intermodal Transport System", *Geoform* 14, pp. 461–469.

destination lacks a direct service, in which case transshipment will be necessary. For example, if cargo originating in an East African port has to be transported to a destination on the Black Sea and no direct service exists between the two regions, then it may be economically justifiable to ship the containerized cargo to the port of Eilat on the Red Sea and move it via the Kedem Landbridge to the port of Ashdod on the Mediterranean, where it will be loaded on to a ship sailing to the Black Sea.

The importance of the NCB, which transfers fewer than 10,000 containers a year, cannot be measured either by the volume of its traffic or by its economic viability when this is narrowly defined. Using either of these criteria, its importance would be quite modest. The Kedem Landbridge, however, is an interesting and important phenomenon. Its importance and its economic rationale depend, not on its ability to compete successfully with an all-water route, as do most existing landbridges in the world, but on its function as an important link in a fully intermodal transport system. The Negev Continental Bridge operation must be evaluated in the light of this wider system. If it contributes to the success of an entire intermodal system, then the profitability of its own operation becomes a secondary consideration.

CHAPTER 7

Logistics and physical distribution

Containerization has helped to improve the productivity of both liner shipping and port operations. The unitization methods, cellular vessels, and gantry cranes have successfully increased the productivity of ship operations and port cargo throughput. With the advancement of intermodal transportation, in which the organization and synchronization of the cargo flow become the central focus of the transportation system, more and more attention and effort have been directed to the necessity of increasing the productivity of the cargo distribution system. For ships, containerization solved the problems of slow turn-around time in port and heavy congestion at the general cargo berth. When large volumes of containerized cargo started flowing into the inland transport networks, the constraints and bottlenecks of the transportation system then shifted to the distribution field. Indeed, the expanded market areas and longer distances over which cargo seemed to move in the new intermodal era also made it necessary to devote more attention to the logistics of moving the goods, the physical distribution of the cargo.

Intermodality, of course, preaches from a total system viewpoint. As mentioned previously, though, the effectiveness of the total chain of transport is measured against the weakest link in the system. Hence, such issues as storage and warehousing, long-haul and short-haul inland distribution, integrated traffic flow, information flow, data processing and documentation — the nuts and bolts of cargo logistics — now rose to the top of the priority list for the various transport modes.

THE CONCEPT OF PHYSICAL DISTRIBUTION

The growing number of firms including a physical distribution department of one form or another in their organizational structure evidenced the increasing significance of the physical distribution element in the total transport system. Although this development may just involve a change in priority for producers, suppliers, or large consumers, which have accommodated a similar function for quite some time, it is a completely new step for the shipping lines and seaport authorities.

Physical distribution has been defined by the American Marketing Association as "the movement and handling of goods from point of production to the point of consumption or use".[1] A more detailed definition views physical distribution as "the management of movement, inventory control, protection, and storage of raw materials and processed or finished goods to and from the production line".[2] Although for some, physical distribution refers only to the operation and management of post-production material flow, and logistics mainly to pre-production material flow, it is the contention here that the two terms — logistics and physical distribution — are synonymous.

Most definitions of physical distribution — or cargo logistics — would agree that the concept is based on four principal components: transportation, marketing, distribution, and management. Each definition follows its own viewpoint, emphasizing a different component and, consequently, placing a different relative weight on each of the four components. Regardless of the specific outlook, however, the transportation element is recognised as the largest single slice in the physical distribution cost pie. This slice, according to many studies, is around one third, though the figure may vary considerably, depending on the nature of the trade, the distance of the trip, and the choice of mode.

The physical distribution concept incorporates under a single management system multiple functions involved in the transport of commodities from producer to consignee, thus enabling clients to receive optimal service, based on their specific needs (Figure 15). The inventory control of consumer products, for example, can be closely coordinated with fluctuations in demand, permitting the maintenance of a low level of stocks and a resultant saving in capital expenditures. In other cases, the location of warehousing may be selected according to a product's trade character-

1. Definitions Committee of the American Marketing Association, 1948 Report.
2. Taff, C.A. (1978), *Management of Physical Distribution and Transportation* (Illinois: Richard D. Irwin).

istics so as to incur minimum transport costs. There may be, too, a considerable saving in packaging costs if the commodities are transported in large units or even in bulk form, thus also achieving economies of scale in transportation costs, and if the final packaging is carried out as close as possible to the consumer's location. In any event, efficient physical distribution systems cannot be achieved without a true command of information flow. For that reason, computerization, data banks, on-line follow-up of cargo flow, automated transport-information services (availability, on the one hand, and customers' requirements, on the other hand) are gradually becoming an integral part of physical distribution management.

Time and space are two important dimensions by which the physical distribution concept should be analysed. From the spatial point of view, one of the principal objectives of physical distribution today is to bridge between the centres of demand and the points of supply of a specific commodity in a rationalized, efficient, and integrated manner. As the global system is composed of an uneven spatial distribution of raw materials, production centres, population distribution, and areas of consumption, efforts must be invested to transfer raw materials, semi-final products, and finished goods to the areas where these are in demand. The transportation industry has been, and still is, a principal component in the effort to overcome the distance between trading centres. Unitization, containerization, and the intermodal concept have come to enhance the importance of managing the total distribution system and to elevate the potential role of physical distribution in the total transport chain.

It is commonly known that, in the long run, cargo will not flow from point of supply (i) to point of demand (j) unless the transportation costs between these two points (C_{ij}) are equal to or lower than the difference in the commodity price between that at the point of demand (P_j) and that at the point of supply (P_i). This relationship may be expressed by the simple equation:

$$C_{ij} \leqslant (P_j - P_j).$$

In a competitive market, in which the market price of a commodity is beyond the control of a single producer, producers will in most cases strive to lower their production costs and to increase their efficiency. As for the remaining component of the equation, transport modes, which are facing bitter competition

PHYSICAL DISTRIBUTION MANAGEMENT

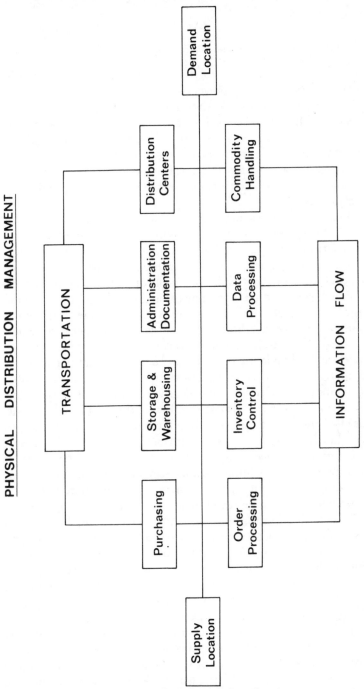

Figure 15. The concept of physical distribution

from both within and outside their specific mode, are certainly doing everything in their power to minimize operating costs; and, indeed, in the last decade they have gone a long way in this direction. Physical distribution, bearing the flag of spatial and economic organization with the objective of coordination and synchronization among producers, transportation modes, and consignees, has greater potential to overcome distances in international and domestic trade, and therefore, to raise efficiency to a new level.

Coordination and synchronization of the cargo flow is to a great extent also concerned with the transport dimension of the physical distribution concept. Obviously, time is a major consideration for shipper, consignee, and transport mode. Reducing travel time, however, does not in itself lubricate all components of the system. Although shorter travel time may bring down the in-transit capital costs of the cargo, the use of faster transport modes is generally assumed to have its additional costs, as well. In an era in which the cost of maintaining high levels of stock is mounting and, therefore, leading many firms to reduce their levels, the parameter of "arrival time" is becoming as significant as that of travel time, if not more so. One of the objectives of physical distribution management is to coordinate the flow of the cargo to the client, based on the fluctuations of demand to which the client is exposed and the changing level of stock at this client's disposal. Physical distribution management can obtain the necessary flexibility of operation by controlling various segments of the cargo flow, including the use of various transport modes, different route combinations, storage warehousing, and stock management.

Physical distribution management is increasingly becoming a key element in the total transport system although currently the discipline is only in its early stages of development. The issue of who will actually control or manage the physical distribution of the cargo remains open, but stands at the forefront of the transport industry and the international trade scene. The range of functions that physical distribution management needs to perform to control and manage integrated traffic flow effectively and efficiently and the extended geographical area that it should cover implies that the concept is outside the scope of small and even many medium-sized firms, that traditionally have maintained special departments for this task under the conventional trading system. If the business of a firm is conducted on a large scale, such as a continent-wide retail store, and it decides to carry out the physical distribution functions within the firm, reorganization will have to take place in order for all the departments involved to adapt themselves to the new functions and dimensions of the physical distribution system under the extended definition of the concept.

Recent experience shows that a great number of firms will have to seek the services of an intermediate party to handle the physical distribution of their commodities. The question of which are the parties striving to handle the various physical distribution functions lies at the heart of the intermodal transport competition. As Chapter 8 explores more closely, sharp competition for control of the cargo throughout its total journey, including the physical distribution segments, currently dominates the transport industry.

One may assume that the shipping lines, which were (and are) the greatest promoters of containerization and intermodality, will involve themselves deeply in physical distribution management too. If land transportation companies find themselves threatened by the increased involvement of the ocean carriers in their own backyard, they may then try to exploit their traditional, and geographical, accessibility to producers and consumers by adding physical distribution management to their operations. Evidence from the activities of some ports, Rotterdam being perhaps the best example, is substantial enough not to rule out the seaports as an active participant in the physical distribution system. Ports may try, and indeed are already trying, to exploit their strategic location and to extend their functions beyond the traditional port boundaries in order to capture their own good share of the intermodal transport trade. Lastly, the other intermediate organizations, such as the international freight forwarders and the NVOCCs, are doing more than just showing interest in the vital physical distribution concept.

INLAND CONTAINER DEPOTS

With the expansion of containerization and the development of intermodality, maritime containers are now penetrating inland more deeply and in larger volumes than ever before. This situation has far-reaching implications for the organization of traffic flow, logistics, and physical distribution. Under the intermodal concept, ocean transportation, ports, land carriers, and physical distribution are seen as individual systems that must closely cooperate and even integrate with one other. One of the most significant manifestations of this trend is the establishment of inland container depots, simply known as inland terminals.

Two principal reasons lie behind the establishment of inland terminals throughout the world: the constant need to improve the efficiency of inland transportation and the ever-growing congestion in the land areas around major ports (and, concomitantly, the lack of available back-up space for handling the increasing volume of container flows). The shifting of the actual handling (i.e., the stuffing and stripping) of seaborne containers to inland locations has two aims: (1) to relieve the congestion constraints of most shoreline urban waterfronts; (2) to extend the continuous flow of container traffic, thus achieving improved economics of cargo distribution by performing the first breaking up of containers closer to the consignee.

The evolution of the inland terminal is partly related to the changes in port operations and the new dimensions of port infrastructure. One of the main objectives of containerization is to reduce the turn-around time of ships in port and, thereby, to increase the throughput of a port's container terminal. Container handling in port, however, is a space-demanding activity. Stuffing and stripping containers cannot be done effectively and efficiently, given the physical layout of conventional break-bulk facilities. The container system requires complete modification and enlargement of this area. At a conventional berth, the ship lies alongside a narrow apron bounded by a storage and transit shed that accommodates all goods not directly loaded from ship to truck or railcars. It is virtually impossible to operate a container system from such a berth. Containers must be accumulated in the port area beforehand to allow their loading once the vessel is in port. Large storage areas are needed to accommodate unloaded containers and for marshalling and manoeuvring containers. The actual amount of space required for a container terminal varies from port to port, depending on several characteristics of the operations: the volume of containers moved, number of containers stripped and stuffed at the terminal itself, average length of stay of containers at the terminal, and storage methods.[3]

Containerization has considerably changed the ratio of berth and back-up area. This may be illustrated by the following example. In the conventional cargo-handling system, it would often take a week to load and unload about 5,000 tons of general cargo. The same berth and back-up space can now handle about twice as much containerized cargo in one day. This implies both a faster loading and unloading system and a much larger back-up area. Many ports have found it difficult, if not impossible, to obtain the necessary space. Ports were traditionally located adjacent to urban areas, and most often the centres of cities. In time, they became bounded by other urban land uses that prevented their immediate inland expansion. Ports unable to obtain new back-up areas are either constrained by the amount of cargo they can handle or forced to relocate some of their activities, perhaps even the entire container operation, to an available space, one that may be considerably inland.

It has happened that even when the necessary space was available, economic and environmental constraints precluded its use by the port. Since the late 1960s, public awareness and concern about the environment and the quality of life have been growing. One expression of this trend is the changing public attitude towards coastal areas and urban waterfronts. The demand by a variety of potential users for land along the shoreline in urban areas has risen constantly since the early 1980s, with an attendant increase in the cost of land. This has placed a serious financial obstacle in the path of ports needing to purchase the land. In 1974, one of the earliest inland container terminals in the United States was established at Butte, Montana, some 900 kilometres inland from Seattle, the harbour it serves. Among other reasons for the construction of this terminal was the cost of land, developed land in Butte selling for $0.20 per square foot compared with $3.00 in the port of Seattle.

Along with a changing public attitude to the waterfront, the demand by ports for expanded terminals and landfills has encountered opposition from environmental and recreational interests. Under the US Coastal Zone Management Act (1972),

3. Hayuth, Y. (1980), "Inland Container Terminal — Function and Rationale", *Maritime Policy and Management* 7, 4, pp. 283–89.

port expansion projects were, and are, carefully re-examined by Federal, state, and local officials. Ports have to submit environmental and economic impact statements before a new project can be approved. Furthermore, some traditional port functions, such as storage and warehousing, began to be challenged and several port communities have encouraged recreational and commercial developments rather than expanded port facilities along the waterfront.

Inland container depots are developing into a vital element in the transport chain. The nature of containerization and intermodality appears favourable for the further evolution of the concept. There is no sign that the demand for coastal areas and urban waterfront by the maritime industry and by recreational interests and other commercial users will ease. On the contrary, public awareness of the city's waterfront lands on the one hand, and port demand for back-up area as a result of the large volumes of containerized cargo moving through the port on the other, will increase the pressure on and the cost of waterfront areas. In addition, the trend towards rationalization of the transport system and the increasing cost of overland transportation should encourage more efficient inland distribution systems for containers — for example, cargo consolidation and large-volume, low-cost unit trains — and thereby enhance the further development of inland terminals.

An integral part of intermodal transportation, inland terminals are an international phenomenon. Having emerged from the developed countries of the West, it has found its way into the developing world as well as into socialist states. In Europe, freight distribution centres and interior transshipment terminals are common phenomena. The railways in the United Kingdom have operated inland clearance depots (ICD) for several decades, but it was only in the early 1970s, with the advent of containerization, that the concept began to flourish. The ICD received operating approval from HM Customs. Such centres, too, are part of Eastern European transportation systems, Poland proving a notable example. They also operate in Asia and South Africa.

Several common locational factors characterize inland intermodal centres. High accessibility to major highways, railways, and seaports is a fundamental constraint for the location of an inland terminal. In addition, it is usually located close to an industrial and commercial centre or to a border-point. The distance of such terminals from seaports, however, may vary considerably, from several kilometres from the port area, as in the case of the joint intermodal centre constructed by the Port of Los Angeles and the Port of Long Beach, to thousands of kilometres from any sea shore, as in the cases of Butte, Montana, and Clearfield, Utah.

Some ports and shipping lines have established intermodal freight stations in the immediate vicinity of the port area, and thereby provide themselves with a short, direct link between the container terminal at the port and the intermodal station. This is meant to achieve a saving in the cost of transferring containers over longer distances. In many cases, however, the operation of an inland container depot in the port area is characterized by heavy congestion, high cost of land, and higher labour costs. When inland terminals are constructed outside the jurisdiction of the longshoremen's union, labour is employed at cheaper rates. Generally, however, the realization of this cost advantage by most ICDs has been difficult because of the lobbying of dock workers, who have resented the trend of losing what they view as their rightful work. The idea of inland container depots in the United States, for instance, was strongly opposed by the unions. The International Longshoremen's Association (ILA), following an agreement won by the International Longshoremen's and Warehousemen's Union (ILWU), added a rule to its contract with the Atlantic Ports' Shipping Association that the longshoremen at US Atlantic and Gulf Coast ports have the sole right to handle, stuff, and strip containers within a 50-mile radius of a port. The "50-mile container rule" has been challenged several times in court, in some cases successfully, in others not, but the full impact of this struggle is still uncertain.

The range of functions of an inland terminal is wide. It may serve as a cargo consolidation and deconsolidation centre, where containers are stuffed or stripped, sorted, packed and transported either to seaports or to other inland destinations. The terminal may serve as a base for customs clearance. It may also be a warehouse and storage area or, very probably, a marshalling yard for containers intended for various modes of transportation and a variety of destinations. A summary of the functions of the inland container depot is presented in Figure 16.

Inland container depots are also termed "inland ports" because they have assumed a significant number of traditional port functions and services; in addition, they have attracted many related services that traditionally were located in the port area. These include shipping-line agents, trucking companies, forwarders, banks, insurance agencies, container-repair facilities, packing firms, and government inspection agencies. In many ways, inland terminals also act as gateways to specific ports. This is certainly the case of the "Port of Butte", in Montana, *vis-à-vis* the Port of Seattle, in Washington. The Butte container terminal is in some respects a distant extension of or complement to Seattle. Under the terms of a working agreement with the Pacific Coast port, Butte is used as a storage, consolidation, and distribution point for containerized cargo on the way to and from Seattle. Butte effectively acts as Seattle's gateway to the United States Mid-West. Inbound cargo does not clear customs at the port of entry, Seattle. Instead, containers are sealed by customs officers at the port and transported over 900 kilometres by rail or truck to Butte, where they are opened for the first time.

A common solution to the need for wide back-up areas and for increasing and speeding cargo throughput was to relocate various port functions to inland terminals, where space was available. One of the most serious obstacles to the through-movement of cargo shipped by means of intermodal transportation and the biggest bottleneck at many container ports, is customs clearance. As the volume of traffic moving through many ports expanded, the slow customs procedures, particularly for less than container loads (LCL), created such congestion that the establishment of inland container depots for this clearance activity became an almost indispensable solution. Great Britain's ICDs, as mentioned earlier in this chapter, are accorded full customs approval. Some of the ICDs are located close to the port area. This is the case, for example, with the ICD at Palmer's Wharf West Quay in South East London, which was commissioned in 1978. Others, such as the Birmingham ICD, are located further inland, close to an industrial centre. ICDs in Britain had an earlier form as customs clearance points for railway ferry wagons, since they offered a more convenient and less costly way of clearing the wagons than did the ports which were sometimes congested. This logic still holds today, as ICDs allow a faster flow of containers through the ports.

The problem of slow customs procedures and red tape is shared by both developing and developed countries. One of the world's largest inland terminals is located in Johannesburg. Containers moving from Durban by unit train in bond are cleared here rather than in the port. Nigeria, which suffered heavily from port congestion in the mid-1970s, constructed a congestion-free inland terminal which houses a resident customs office about 50 kilometres from the port of Lagos.

One of the important functions of an inland terminal is to consolidate shipments: the grouping of consignments with different origins and destinations into larger units, like full container loads, for the next leg of the journey. This function may benefit both small and large shippers. For the former, especially if located away from the port area, an inland consolidation centre can minimize transportation costs by exploiting the economy of movements of full container loads. Since many inland terminals are located close to industrial or commercial centres, containers arriving from the port can be stripped near the point of delivery and, perhaps more importantly, go through customs inspection at the point of their final discharge. A consolidation centre located close to the port area has the advantage of performing its function with lower property costs and under less congested conditions than would be the case in the port itself. Such a centre can deconsolidate containers arriving from different overseas origins, dispatch consignments intended for the local area, and consolidate shipments bound for inland destinations — obtaining, in the process, higher utilization of the containers and a saving on transportation costs.

Consolidation is a prime function of the inland depots in France, which are operated by individual shipping lines, and of the inland terminals in Toronto, Winnipeg, Edmonton, and Calgary, which are owned either by the Canadian National Railway or the Canadian Pacific Railway. Nei Li, an inland terminal situated in the heart of Taiwan's northern industrial zone, has excellent accessibility to both the northern port of Keelung and the southern port of Kaoshiung; a major consolidation centre, this ICD also contains a customs branch office and many shipper-related services. In Poland, a central agency, PSK, has full control over container movements within the country, including the consolidation of containers. The

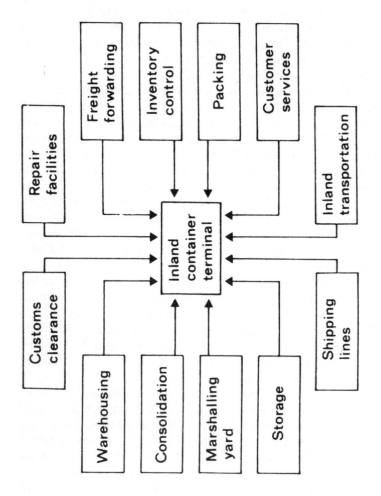

Figure 16. Functional structure of inland container terminals
Source: Hayuth, Y., *Maritime Policy and Management*, 7 (1980), p. 289.

agency, together with the Polish State Railways, has established a series of inland container depots in such strategically located inland cities as Warsaw, Poznan, Lodz, and Krakow.

One of the most significant contributions of strategically located inland container terminals is their furthering of the fast moving of a high-volume long intermodal journey. A fast, large container-ship and the speedy handling of its containers at the port will not yield the ultimate advantage of large-scale intermodal movements if the cargo cannot reach its inland destination at the same rapid pace. Inland terminals thus help extend far into the interior the economies of scale from concentrated, single linear flows.

Inland terminals were established not only as a result of the need for space, but also as part of a new concept in physical distribution and the changing role of the ocean carrier in the framework of the origin-to-destination journey that developed with containerization. Cargo could now penetrate the interior with relative ease, moving in containers hundreds and even thousands of miles from port of discharge to final destination. With such expanded hinterlands, economic and logistical justifications obtain for establishing regional marketing depots that would serve not only a local area but a whole region and that would combine several normally separate functions, such as inventory control, transportation management, and packaging. The specific advantages of a regional marketing depot may be illustrated by the example of Freeport Center in Clearfield, Utah, one of the largest inland distribution centres in the United States.

Clearfield Freeport Center, a former naval supply depot, occupies a pivotal location, at the junction of major railroads and highways. It can offer second-day delivery to the entire West Coast market, from the State of Washington in the north to California in the south. Goods may also be held at Freeport Center for any purpose without being subject to inventory tax of any kind. Imports and exports may clear customs here, away from the congestion and high costs of coastal ports. The centre allows large distributors to reduce the cost of local delivery. Finally, it saves transportation costs by offering full-container-load (FCL) rates and eliminating secondary transportation.

An inland regional marketing depot can also ease one of the most difficult and wasteful problems of container transportation

— the empty leg. A truck that carries a loaded container from the port to an inland destination quite often returns to the port carrying an empty box. An inland regional depot can shorten this empty leg by providing cargo intended for the port. Most often, too, the truck owner will agree to carry the return-voyage goods at a reduced rate.

In developing countries, physical distribution management is hampered by the lack of an inland traffic infrastructure; for this reason, the adoption of the new cargo-handling methods is generally limited to areas relatively close to ports. In such countries, inland container depots must be accompanied by improved road or railway links in order to exploit the benefits of door-to-door service beyond the coastal regions. Only then may an inland terminal serve as an extension of a port and as a regional marketing centre. There are signs, nevertheless, that the physical distribution concept will take hold in developing countries. The most prominent example, perhaps, is the inland terminal currently under construction in Kano, a city in northern Nigeria, some 750 miles from the coast. The Kano terminal is a joint venture between a British shipping company (Ocean Transport and Trading Ltd. of Liverpool) and a Nigerian investment group. The shipping company's rationale is that this terminal will provide an inland distribution and collection system that will expand the line's tributary area and improve the utilization and turn-around of its capital-intensive, large containerships, which call at a limited number of ports. The Kano terminal is intended as a regional container centre for northern Nigeria; longer-term plans call for Kano to serve as a distribution centre for cargo bound for Niger, which borders northern Nigeria. Currently, this cargo is routed through the port of Contonou in Dahomey.

CHAPTER 8

Competition and complementarity

A CONCEPTUAL OVERVIEW

Intermodality has significantly altered the conventional nature of transport competition. Many of the basic rules of and the rationale for the single-mode approach in transportation that preceded intermodal development are either obsolete or in need of major revision. In any event, many of the commonly accepted assumptions relating to transport competition just two decades ago may not survive the test of time simply because, with the intermodal concept, "the ball game" is different.

Perhaps the most fundamental change that intermodality has introduced into the transport industry is the shift of focus from the traditional point-to-point transport practice — i.e., port-to-port or station-to-station service — to a through system, from the cargo's origin to its final destination. In this latter system, control of the cargo is the key element. Indeed, whoever controls the cargo throughout the entire intermodal system — whether this involves ships, trains, trucks, and/or seaports — has a competitive edge over anyone who exercises control in but single transport modes. The party controlling the cargo throughout can make all the decisions, from the selection of route, carrier, port of call, to the transport mode or modes. Such control also relieves shippers of their traditional concern, and input, regarding specific routes, ports, storage facilities, and cargo-handling capabilities. It is conceivable that in the near future, transport modes will alter their conventional marketing strategies in regard to the central element of the competition — cargo control.

The increased specialization of the transportation modes required by the intermodal system and the different organizational structures of transporting international trade have sharpened intermodal, as well as intra-modal, transport competition. The potential hinterland of each transport mode (as seen in Chapter 6) has been stretched, and the spatial and functional range of operation of the transportation segments, whether maritime or land transportation, has been extended, sometimes beyond the conventional barriers. Transport elements have thus been exposed to more competition in their traditionally dominant areas, and more transport modes are competing within an enlarged market place available to them.

Furthermore, as the rules within the transportation arena have changed with intermodality, new players have entered the competition. Although none is a new face in the transport industry, their appearance and involvement in specific trade routes or within a certain distance range are certainly new. In the pre-container era, the ocean carrier's primary concern and responsibility were usually confined to cargo handling, vessel steaming, and cargo discharging. In the intermodal system, the ocean carrier often adds the land transportation segment to its own operation and responsibility; thus, it enters into direct competition with the railroads. The extent of this phenomenon during the mid-1980s was indeed new.

River transport is one of the oldest modes in the transportation industry. It is only in the last decade, however, with the introduction of barge containerization, that this mode has become a competitor for the general cargo trade. On the trade route from Rotterdam to the heart of Europe, the railroads and truck companies usually, and mainly, confined competition with the barge carriers to bulk commodities. Now, Rhine River barges, fully loaded with containers, constitute a serious competitor to railroads and trucks on this route. Another newcomer to intermodal competition is air transportation, and airfreight is gradually carving its own niche in international trade. Shipping lines complain that air transportation is skimming off the cream of their cargo, in terms of its value rather than in terms of traffic volume. Finally, among the newer entrants to this transport competition, special attention should be drawn to the non-vessel operating common carriers (NVOCCs). Intermodality provides NVOCCs with favourable conditions for success in the fray, particularly in the critical element of cargo control.

Intermodality has introduced not only intensification, new players, and new rules to the competitive transport environment, it has also strengthened the element of complementarity. Once again, this is true for both intermodal and intra-modal transportation. Railroads and truck operators began to find it increasingly beneficial to cooperate and coordinate their services on a complementary basis. On the intra-modal level, rail piggyback operation, which primarily serves the local market, and ISO container trains, which principally serve the international trade, were placed under growing pressure to complement their services in order to ensure increased efficiency and an improved balance in their trade routes. Perhaps, though, the most significant manifestation of the need for complementarity in the new transport environment is the formation of the total, or multimodal, transport company — a company that operates and controls a combination of modal services.

In the United States, all the trends described above and brought about by intermodality were accompanied by the deregulation of the transportation industry. Truck, railway, water, and air transportation had all been regulated and monitored by different governmental organizations; each, with its own area of responsibility, tried to discourage cooperation and coordination between and within the transport modes, based on the assumption that such cooperation would inhibit competition. This assumption has proven wrong. A century of coming up against a rigid, regulated environment, although provided with some relaxation through the Transportation Act of 1940, reduced the level of competition in the United States transport industry and caused a degree of stagnation, certainly in the railroad system. Moreover, one of the prime reasons for the US Government's decision to deregulate the industry was to enhance competition, and, indeed, the transportation modes have responded in this direction after a relatively short period of adjustment. Competition, as well as complementarity, between and within the transport modes has flourished since deregulation.

Obviously, the deregulation of transportation was a major catalyst for intermodality. Without the freedom, although somewhat restricted, to cooperate, select routes, merge, enter new services, or operate in a spatially expanded market place, intermodality could not have developed. Certainly the transport industry would not have evidenced such a large-scale involvement and long-term commitment to intermodality as it currently appears to have done.

The basic criteria that determined the selection of a specific carrier by the shipper and decided the structure of the modal split of the cargo movement have not changed with intermodality. Transport costs and quality of transport services have remained the key factors on the basis of which the decisions regarding transport selection are being made. On the other hand, alteration of the emphasis and relative significance of the variables within these two closely related criteria has occurred. The traditional cost-comparison analysis, based on individual segments of the transport journey, must now be modified to an analysis of the total system. From this point of view, the relative advantages of individual modes may have shifted, depending obviously on the nature of each trade route. Also, some of the conventional parameters that determine the quality of transport services have received new dimensions. In the intermodal area, the criteria of speed, flexibility, and availability were raised in significance and meaning because the range of possibilities in these parameters was enormously expanded.

The basic characteristics of the individual transport modes have not been changed either. Water and rail transportation, which have to endure a high proportion of fixed costs, have, and always had, an advantage on long-distance hauls, while trucks, which offer more flexible operations, maintain an edge with short-distance trips. Intermodality did not change this basic pattern. Important modifications in the effective operating range of each transport mode, however, did alter some of the commonly accepted rules of transport competition. For centuries, it was a basic belief that water transportation was the cheapest mode of transportation, and thus attempts were made to extend the ocean voyage as deep into the interior as possible through river navigation. In fact, a traditional criterion for port location was the furthest interior point that a sea-going vessel could reach. Although this assumption is maintained even now, its validity has been made conditional. On certain trade routes and on some segments of the trip, an inland transport mode can compete successfully with water transportation; on a macro level, the development of landbridges provides an example (see Chapter 6). On the macro level, the relocation of many ports from their inland location to the mouth of the estuary means, among other things, meeting containerized ocean-borne cargo as soon as it reaches the shoreline — quite in contrast to port location criteria just two decades ago.

LAND AND WATER TRANSPORTATION

Intermodal transportation has brought about a major challenge, as well as opportunities, for shipping lines involved in the container trade. As intermodal movements grow in volume, shipping companies have been faced with the need to expand their operations beyond their traditional at-sea responsibilities. Although container lines had been involved in the overland movement of their cargo for some years, the development of intermodal transport greatly accelerated and intensified the involvement of the shipping lines in the land transportation leg.

For the liner operator participating in the container transport trade, the pressure to increase traffic volume has mounted as containerization and intermodal transport developed. With regard to freight rates, the liner operator is quite restricted: by market conditions, overtonnaging in the prime trade routes and stiff competition, and even by the liner conferences. On the other hand, the capital investment of this operator is enormous, surpassing by far that required by the conventional liner operator. In addition, the much larger present-day containerships, compared with the first, second, or even third generation of container vessels, demand the utmost effort from their operators to increase the load factor of each vessel.

Since the level of freight rates is to a great extent beyond the operator's control, as are some operating costs like fuel prices, the only road open to the liner operator to increase cargo volumes is to modify and improve marketing efforts. Shipping lines participating in intermodal trade could not overlook the fact that, being the major initiators and promoters of intermodal movements, they had an initial advantage over other transport modes as far as cargo control was concerned. Under these circumstances, it was only natural that shipping lines began to penetrate more aggressively the inland transportation market, beyond their traditional operating arena.

The railway–steamship relationship exhibits one of the most remarkable changes that have taken place in the current development of intermodalism. A determination of whether competition or complementarity best describes the nature of their relationship depends greatly on one's point of view. On the one hand, the increased involvement of shipping lines in inland transportation may be looked upon as direct competition with the railroads. How else can one view the heavy investments of the American President Intermodal Company in railcars? In the background was the fear on the part of the railroads that steamship operators would not limit their inland transport involvement to the international trade market. Recent attempts by shipping lines calling at US West Coast ports to complement their unbalanced eastbound international container traffic with westbound domestic container movements illustrate just how realistic were these concerns. The railways' long-time partner was now becoming their competitor.

On the other hand, the railway–steamship alliance of the early and mid-1980s did produce significant trunk routes crossing the United States, thus generating for the railroads business that otherwise would never have existed. The employment of dedicated unit trains and double-stack container cars by Sea-Land, APL, and other steamship lines brought with it additional cargo traffic for inland transportation, although not all of it fell into the hands of the railroads. This cargo, or at least part of it, comes at the expense of the all-water Panama Canal route, or in direct competition with the United States Lines' large container vessels.

Up to now, in the critical competition for control of the cargo, it seems that the steamship has had the edge over any of the inland transport modes. Shipping companies have promoted intermodal traffic, heavily invested in intermodal handling and transporting equipment, and acquired their own inland transportation services. Currently it is they that are best equipped and positioned in the intermodal system to handle and control "door-to-door" service. It is difficult to predict, however, whether this situation will prevail in the future. The attempt in 1986 by the American railroad giant CSX to take over Sea-Land has put yet another question mark on this issue. It may be an exceptional action or it may herald a reversal of which side holds the competitive edge.

INLAND TRANSPORTATION

Railroads and trucks were the traditional principal carriers of overland general cargo trade in Europe and in the United States. Their relationship has had ups and downs over the past century. Until the Second World War, the dominance of the railroads over trucks in inland transport movements, particularly in the United States, was clear. With major construction of highway networks after World War II, however, the advantage tilted towards the road hauliers, particularly on short-distance trips of up to 500 kilometres and in the general cargo trade. During the 1960s and most of the 1970s, the balance of power between these two modes stabilized — or stagnated as some would have it. It was the advent of intermodality and, particularly, the deregulation of the transport industry in the United States in 1980 that shook up both modes, forcing them both to re-evaluate their positions in the changing environment of the transport industry. The railroads were provided the opportunity to strengthen their advantages, particularly with regard to traffic volumes and long-distance trips, and thus to re-enter, if not forge ahead in, the competition for the general cargo trade.

The railroad industry itself is also characterized by intra-modal competition. There are at least four different ways of transporting containers by rail:

1. Container on a flat car (COFC), where ISO containers are lifted onto flat rail cars and then, at the other end of the trip, put on a truck for hauling to final destination.

2. The swap-body system, common on the European scene, where the truck body is lifted off the chassis, transported by rail to another truck chassis, attached and then hauled to final destination.

3. Trailer on a flat car (TOFC), where semi-trailers are loaded on flat rail cars, transported by rail to a point, then picked up by tractor for final delivery. This is commonly referred to as the piggyback system.

4. Double-stack container cars, the latest development in rail intermodality, where two containers are stacked one on the other in specially designed rail cars.

The first and the last systems are primarily used by international intermodal transportation, while the other two systems mainly serve the domestic trade. The growing traffic in domestic containerization, however, has raised the debate within the industry with regard to the mixing of domestic and international traffic; proponents see mixing as ensuring better utilization of the equipment and improving the cargo-flow balance on the main trade routes.

In Europe, road transportation holds a stronger position *vis-à-vis* the railroads than it does in the United States. The relatively short distances and the high density of highway networks in Europe better fit the inherent advantage of truck flexibility. Then, too, road transportation in Europe competes against a politically fragmented railroad industry, despite measures of cooperation between individual national railroads. European truck operators, however, may find this competition increasingly difficult in the coming years. Governments will continue to support and protect their national railroads, particularly if more investment in new equipment will be necessary. European railroads are already attempting to increase their competitiveness on shorter distances, and it is possible that the break-even point between railroads and trucks on certain routes will be reduced from the current 400 kilometres. The trucking industry, for its part, will most likely be constrained in attempts to increase the permissible axle weight and trailer dimensions because of already restricting road-transport regulations and ever-growing highway congestion. In addition, road transportation is currently confronting an old, but in some ways also a new, competitor for the general container trade: inland waterways.

The inland waterway system was the transport mode slowest to adapt itself to containerization and intermodality. Just a decade ago, the barge container was a rare sight on the Rhine. The reasons for this were threefold. First, the image of an old and unreliable service accompanied inland waterways. Secondly, the low speed of the barges (having the slowest transit time of the transport modes) was a drawback. The average transit time for the 350-kilometre route along the Rhine was seven hours for truck haulage, 15 hours for express freight train, 20—25 hours for downstream barge navigation, and 35–40 hours for upstream barge movement. Thirdly, the extra handling, lack of transport equipment, and unreliability in performing a door-to-door operation were also disadvantages in moving containers by river transport.

The 1980s began to witness a breakthrough for the inland water transport of containers. In 1977 an estimated 40,000 TEU were carried on the Rhine; in 1982, the traffic volume reached the 100,000 TEU level; and by 1985, more than 200,000 TEU were transported on the Rhine. Parallel to this increase in the volume of containers, a network of more than 20 specialized inland terminals was constructed along the Rhine, and the prospect is for additional growth. The explanation for the sudden flourishing of container trade on the inland waterways of Europe lies in the low cost; congestion-free movements; seven-days-a-week service (i.e., without any of the restrictions imposed on highway truck movements, such as those during the weekends in Germany); the ability to transport in almost all weather conditions, day and night; favourable operating conditions from the environmental point of view; and much improved transfer facilities.

In the United States, despite the deregulation of barge lines in 1983, truck operators participating in intermodal movements are not worried as much about the inland waterways as a potential competitor because the barges are occupied mostly with bulk commodities. The main concern of the US trucking industry is being able to establish its own role in the intermodal system. The confrontation of road transportation with the intermodal concept came hand-in-hand with the exposure of hauliers to the deregulated environment.

The motor carriers pursue two parallel strategies in order to win a share of the intermodal market. One strategy is to improve their competitive position *vis-à-vis* the other transport modes; another is to search for means of cooperation, partnerships, and complementary service agreements with the competitive modes. In their competition with the railroads for the intermodal market in the new deregulated environment, the truck operators are aiming not only to exploit their inherent edge in the short-distance range, but also to search anew for any relative advantages or available opportunities in the medium-range distances. These may include the use of high-cube trailers, 48 feet long and 102 inches wide; and entering into specialized commodity trades that necessitate specialized hauling equipment, such as tank containers. The tendency of shipping lines to concentrate their traffic in load centres, moreover, has opened up opportunities for short and medium-distance hauls by inland feeder services. There is, finally, a growing trend among motor carriers in one region to compete with those in another region in order to have accessibility to a wider market.

Truck operators, however, did not withdraw entirely from the competition on long-distance hauls, despite being at a disadvantage compared to the railroads and their double-stack trains. Truckers offer direct service on irregular routes and to locations not accessible to the main rail corridors, such as rural areas and suburbs, which otherwise would need a truck connection from a railroad station; the long-distance hauliers emphasize their faster transit time in these cases. Another survival strategy in the long-distance trade is to obtain control, by official agreement, of a specific trade between one port abroad, say, in Central or South America, and the United States. This is a particularly interesting method because obtaining control of the cargo as early as its point of origin is one of the most effective ways to ensure a place in the intermodal trade.

In the changing market place, motor carriers also pursue the way of complementarity rather than competition with other modes. Truck operators may view, and in certain cases rightly, the piggyback movements as a complementary operation with the railroads. Since motor carriers have an advantage with regard to equipment positioning by being, for instance, more flexible than are railroads in the search for return cargo on the weak leg of a trade route, trucking firms may cooperate with shipping lines operating in, say, the Pacific trade in order to complement their relatively weak westbound traffic.

NVOCC

It was logical to predict that even with the advance of intermodal transportation, the competition between and within the principal traditional segments of international trade — ocean transportation, land transportation, and seaports strategically located between them — would continue to prevail although in a different manner. A new organizer of transport services, however, did emerge. Known as NVOCC, it became a new competitive factor on the intermodal transport scene.

NVOCCs came into existence as developers of land and water intermodal traffic. In 1961, the United States Federal Maritime Commission established the designation "non-vessel-operating common carrier by water" (NVOCC) to denote a person or organization that provides international transportation on an intermodal basis, issues through intermodal bills of lading, and assumes liability just like the owner of a ship on which cargo is carried. Although the NVOCCs do not own vessels, they use the vessels of other companies.[1] During the first decade or so of their appearance, the NVOCCs were constrained by the strictly regulated environment that characterized the United States transport system. It was, though, precisely this environment, which also constrained the operation of domestic and international freight forwarders, that had much to do with the very phenomenon of NVOCCs.

From their inception, the NVOCCs have faced difficulties, particularly with the US Interstate Highway Commission (ICC), which prevented them from filing through joint rates with surface carriers. Accordingly, they did not receive appropriate attention from other transport modes, which for the most part witnessed their appearance passively. An exception were liner operators, who under pressure to keep their load factors high, did deal with the NVOCCs by selling them vessel space. While the containership operators were busy digesting the ever-changing market place and the land transportation modes were reoccupied with the newly deregulated environment that descended on them, the NVOCCs, now also relieved of many of their previous constraints, started to proliferate in the intermodal trade market and gradually win the trust of shippers, not only in the United States but also in many other countries, including the Soviet Union.

Although one may claim that an NVOCC is just another version of the conventional freight forwarder, in fact its capabilities and potential impact on liner operators and on the nature of intermodal competition are far greater. The NVOCCs are very well positioned in the intermodal system. If containerization is primarily a set of technological innovations, intermodality is first of all an organizational "creature". This is exactly the character of the NVOCC, which is an organizationally oriented service. In addition, one of the most effective strategies for improving competitive position in the intermodal system, as has been noted, is to gain control of the cargo. Controlling the cargo was exactly one of the main objectives of the NVOCCs since they began offering their services, and to do so they do not have to alter their marketing policies as much as the other modes do. NVOCCs, which neither own any transport equipment nor operate any vehicles or vessels, are not tied to a rigid transport

1. Mahoney, J. H. (1985), *Intermodal Freight Transportation* (Westport: ENO Foundation for Transportation), p. 80.

infrastructure and ever-changing rolling stock; consequently, they are not burdened with the enormous capital costs that other transport modes have to endure. Nor do they have any commitment to a specific trade route or conference. Hence, they can offer a shipper the widest choice of transport routes and the most flexible arrangements of intermodal transportation. They can set up routes and quote their own freight rates. Moreover, in the over-capacity condition of most containerized routes, the NVOCC should not have many problems in obtaining cargo space from shipping companies on a contract basis.

By thus positioning themselves between the shipper and the carrier, the NVOCCs break an old tradition of direct contact between shipper and shipping company in the sale of cargo space on vessels. The new pattern makes it even more difficult for the liner operator to obtain control of the cargo. It is only a matter of a short time — if, indeed, it has not already occurred — before the carriers realize that the NVOCC, once their client, has become their competitor.

SEA – AIR TRANSPORT COMPETITION

Air freight is one of the fastest growing segments of the airline industry, and has become an integral part of the world economy and the international trade scene. Until the 1970s, air freight was not recognized as a meaningful competitor of ocean transport for international trade or of surface transport for domestic trade. Aircargo was treated as a stepchild of air-passenger transport, and it is still far from being recognized by shippers and freight forwarders as an independent, self-sustained mode of transport. Admittedly, the all-cargo air carriers were for many years greatly constrained by the lack of economically operating aircraft. The introduction into service of the wide-body jets, particularly the Boeing 747, the major improvements of aircargo terminals, and the growing recognition of the tremendous potential of airlines as a freight transport mode, able to handle containers and standardized equipment, have all combined to upgrade the competitive ability of air transportation. In 1976, about 9.3 million tons of freight were carried by air, and 21,540 million freight ton-kilometres were performed. In 1985, these figures climbed to 13.2

million tons of freight handled on international and domestic air routes and 39,310 million freight ton-kilometres performed.[2]

Competition for passengers between air and surface transport on long-range routes was decided very much in favour of the former mode with the introduction of the Boeing 707 and the DC-8 jets at the end of the 1950s. As for airborne cargo traffic, despite its present growth, the share of air transport in the total volume of international trade is very small, at present accounting for less than 1% of total international cargo movements. In terms of value, however, aircargo represents 10–20% of the international trade, depending on the trade route involved. The competitive advantages of air transport over surface modes, land and ocean transport, with regard to freight can be illustrated by discussing four main factors: time, cost, nature of the cargo, and market characteristics.

Short transit time is one of the major advantages of air transport, particularly for medium and long hauls. This advantage derives, obviously, from the high speed of the aircraft; however, there are other contributory factors. The time-saving factor is particularly significant if the transit time is considered to be the total time of moving a consignment from origin to final destination. In cases in which these points are inland locations, airports are often closer and more accessible to the markets than are seaports. When a comparison is made of door-to-door transit times, the use of air transport as the cargo-carrying mode must be compared to the combined transport time of land and sea transport plus the time needed at the break-of-bulk points. In these cases, the time saved by using air transport on medium or long hauls is most meaningful.

Another aspect of total cargo transit time is the frequency of transport services. The number of flights per week, or per month, available to cargo shippers in most large trade centres is considerably greater than the sailing frequencies of liner ships. Moreover, the transfer of air freight from one flight to another is faster than the equivalent move between two sea-going vessels. Although containerization has greatly reduced the time for ocean transshipment, current improvements in ground facilities at airports and the use of special containers as well as other unitized cargo handling methods for aircraft still leave the time gap much in favour of air transport.

2. *ICAO Bulletin*, 1986.

Speed of transport is not just an advantage, it is a vital consideration for several groups of commodities:[3]

(a) Products possessing the biological constraint of a short lifespan and which must, therefore, reach the market in a fresh condition, such as some flowers, fruits like strawberries, and fresh meat. Because of their sensitivity to the length of a voyage, these products have no alternative but to use air transport for medium and long distances.

(b) Commodities with a short economic life span, whether items shipped for a specific occasion, like Christmas, or fashions that must reach their market at a certain time in order not to lose value.

(c) Consignments for which air transport acts primarily as a marketing tool, enabling the meeting of a sudden, unexpected pick-up in the demand for a product or of an opportunity in certain markets for specific products.

(d) Emergency shipments, such as a machine urgently needed for a shut-down production line or medicines and first-aid equipment. This group also includes commodities sent by air on a one-time basis because of problems encountered in the usual surface modes, such as strikes or sailing-time delays, and the need to meet a supply deadline in order to maintain reliability.

(e) Commodities whose fast supply by air allows a reduction in the level of stocks maintained, thus enabling considerable capital savings. Spare parts also fall into this group.

(f) Products whose faster integration into production justifies the higher transport costs of sending them air freight. If a certain machine can be moved into production one month earlier, the income generated during this time may well be much higher than the additional transport cost.

(g) For high-value items, a short transit time, even though incurring higher freight rates, may save considerably on the in-transit capital cost of an item, and so reduce the time gap between payment for a consignment and offering it for sale.

3. Hayuth, Y. (1983), "The Evaluation and Competitiveness of Air Cargo Transportation: The Case of Israel's Airborne Trade", *Transport Reviews* 3, pp. 265–286.

Cost factors constitute a second parameter affecting competition. The high cost of air freight represents one of its major constraints. In a line haul cost comparison, air transport costs more than does any other mode. The main reasons for this situation are the higher capital expenses of airplanes in relation to their carrying capacity and the relatively high fuel costs of operating aircraft. The freight rate gap is wide when IATA tariffs are applied, narrower when tariffs are based on charter operations. On the basis of an overall cost comparison, on the other hand, and not only the line haul cost, air transport is not always found to be the most expensive mode. The total distribution system, from origin to final destination, includes a list of cost elements, such as packaging, insurance, pick up and delivery, and capital costs. Air transport has an advantage over ocean transport in many of these elements. For example, the faster trip and the more delicate handling of the cargo allow air freight to be protected by lighter packaging than the solid, seaworthy crates used in ocean transport. This packaging differentiation can be translated into various savings — on labour, materials, cargo weight, and volume — which when combined can be reflected in lower overall transport costs. Again, it may be true that containerization has greatly reduced packaging costs for seaborne trade; however, air freight still holds a distinct advantage when it comes to certain machinery, that may be, and often is, transported by air on a pallet, with no packaging at all. Related to the packaging advantage — but at the other end of the trip — is the cost of product refurbishing, which is lower in air freight. Automobiles shipped in airplanes, to take one example, do not require the protective grease layer applied to withstand an ocean voyage.

Insurance rates are another area in which air freight has the advantage. Today's aircraft are extremely reliable. Statistics indicate that many more accident-free miles are performed by airplanes than by any other form of transport. Because, too, of the shorter time the cargo is in transit, along with the low rate of cargo damage and spoilage, the insurance rates assessed on air freight on a particular route are considerably lower than those applicable in ocean transport. In many cases, shippers of air freight insure their consignments with a "total loss" type of policy, which is considerably cheaper than the "all risk" insurance customarily used in sea transport.

The locational advantage of airports with respect to markets, discussed earlier in terms of time savings, also represents significant cost benefits. On the basis of a complete door-to-door service, particularly if an inland origin or destination point is involved, the air freight cost must be compared with the combined cost of sea transport, land transport, and the added terminal handling.

The characteristics of the cargo constitute the major determining factor in a decision on the suitability of a consignment for shipment by air or by sea. Traditionally, air freight has been characterized by its high value, perishability, small size, fragility, and high-priority status. The growth of the air transport industry, in general, and the growing dimensions of the wide-body aircraft, in particular, have enabled freight to expand beyond these traditional qualities as it has penetrated new markets. And, indeed, the degree of penetration of air freight into the international trade scene is well illustrated by the range of commodities that currently travel by air.

Nevertheless, the high-value commodity still remains one of the main characteristics of air freight and has represented an area of increasing concern to ocean shipping companies. In US foreign trade, for example, air freight in 1975 skimmed off one fifth of the revenue of maritime liner companies although it took away only a negligible share of their tonnage.[4] The traditional reasons for shipping high-value cargo by air are the need for careful handling and safe transport. Additionally, goods with a high unit value can bear a higher transport cost more easily than can an item with a low unit value. For example, an air freight rate of $1,000 per ton imposed on a consignment having a value of $10,000 per ton represents 10% of the cargo value. The same freight imposed on an item valued at $2,500 per ton constitutes 40% of the product value, a high additional cost that the market cannot always bear. In the past few years, various aspects of capital cost have also become important factors, as will be elaborated.

Perishables (fresh produce and items with the biological constraint of a short shelf life) have, in many cases, no choice but to use air transport to reach a market. On medium and long-distance trades, air transport is perhaps the only feasible mode for such commodities.

4. Sletmo, G. K. and Williams, E. W. (1981), *Liner Conferences in the Container Age* (New York: Macmillan).

The density of a consignment or, as more commonly expressed in the transport industry, the stowage factor may determine the air freight eligibility of a cargo. The chargeable unit of freight for the various modes of transport depends on the ratio between the load and the volume capacity of the transport mode. For a ship, the major constraint of its design lies in volume, not weight. For an aircraft — in theory, at least — weight, not volume, is the primary design constraint. Accordingly, air transport tariffs are generally quoted on a per unit of weight basis and ocean shipping tariffs, on a per volume of cargo basis. These differences in the calculation of freight rates between air and sea transport illustrate the relative advantages of each of the modes with regard to the stowage factor of the cargo. Shippers of high-density (and lower value) cargo will generally find it more economical to choose sea transport. Air freight, on the other hand, can be very competitive for low-density cargo. A chargeable unit in air freight is normally 1,000 kilograms or seven cubic metres (245 cubic feet). Volume does not become a factor in the cost of air freight until it exceeds seven cubic metres. In ocean transport, by contrast, the chargeable unit is either 1,000 kilograms or one cubic metre, whichever is larger. For general cargo commodities, because of their stowage factor, the freight rate is charged in most cases on the basis of volume, not weight. Thus, if the chargeable unit cost to ship a quantity of general cargo weighing one ton and occupying seven cubic metres of volume by sea is $80 and the chargeable unit to ship the same consignment to the same destination by air is $500, it will be cheaper to use air transport.

The use of containers somewhat improves the competitive situation of ocean transport because then the weight-volume ratio as a basis for calculating the freight rate is not one ton or one cubic metre, as previously mentioned, but one ton or 1.75 cubic metres. (The inside volume of a 20-foot standard marine container is 30.5 cubic metres, and the carrying capacity is about 17 – 18 tons.)

The choice of air freight over surface transport turns, to a great extent, on the prevailing market environment and the specific market characteristics of every item. In general, the growth of air freight traffic is highly correlated with the growth of world economic activity. In a world economy informed by high rates of inflation and expensive costs of capital, the economic conditions reveal several important advantages possessed by air freight over other transport modes. First, air transport can present a considerable saving in capital costs. As companies are forced to reduce their level of inventory, the speed and high frequency of air transport reduce the lead time involved in moving a product to market, allowing producers and importers to maintain a continuous flow of merchandise with a low level of stock. The saving in inventory costs and accompanying warehousing expenses can be significant. Moreover, the shorter duration of transport from door to door means, in effect, that less capital is tied up during the transit of the merchandise, when no profit can be received. The longer the transport and the more valuable the goods, the higher is the capital investment.

Secondly, air transport offers greater flexiblity, being better able to meet special market requirements and to respond more quickly to any changes in market characteristics. In a fluctuating and unpredictable market, it is very difficult for shippers to meet a sudden increase in demand because orders filled through ocean transport are based on expected demand for several weeks or months. Air freight, by contrast, provides a trade-off between higher transport cost and continuous reliability of service. Certain products may face a higher demand in a certain market at a specific time. In some cases, the demand can be expected, such as for some commodities during the Christmas season; but in other cases, an unpredicted gap in supply to a market offers the possibility of either a potential profit, if the cargo is delivered on time, or a possible loss, if the commodities reach the market after the demand peaks.

The higher freight rates for air freight are, then, considered an opportunity cost. Seasonal markets, emergency demand, off-season sale opportunities, and the shipment of small quantities constitute still other market opportunities for which air freight may provide an advantage. Of course, users of air freight (unlike users of sea transport, who can in emergency turn to air) have no fallback for urgent consignments if there are disruptions or delays.

A distribution of commodities by mode of transportation will show three different groups.

AIR TRANSPORT "CAPTIVE" CARGO

This group consists of items for which the air transport mode is very clearly the dominant mode of transportation. Included in the list are live plants, flowers, strawberries, leather and fur goods, works of art, and antiques. Two main characteristics of these items immediately stand out: high value or a high rate of perishability.

SEABORNE "CAPTIVE" CARGO

This group includes items for which sea transport is clearly the dominant mode. Bulk cargoes — grains, minerals, chemicals, ores, oil — are obviously an important part of this group, but steel, logs, cement, and cotton are also included. Seaborne "captive" cargo is characterized either by large volume, which can be accommodated only by a ship, or by physical dimensions that cannot fit into the limited capacity of an aircraft.

ROUTINE SURFACE-DIVERTIBLE TRAFFIC

This group consists of a wide variety of items that could utilize either of the two transport modes, but over which no one mode has a dominant share. This group proves the most difficult to define, and the complexity of factors involved in the choice of transport mode for every item only complicates any attempt to characterize the commodities within the group. Cost factors constitute, perhaps, the principal consideration in this category; whereas the speed factor and the physical characteristics of the commodity, which are significant for many items in the first two groups, are secondary or incidental considerations. Nevertheless, the commodities falling into this group, and not the perishable/emergency class of goods as one may have expected, comprise the greatest portion of air freight traffic today.

In a case study attempting to analyse the factors affecting the choice between air and sea transport for their freight, exporters, importers, and freight forwarders were requested to list, in rank order, the factors considered important in their decision-making process regarding freight transport mode choice.[5] The most frequent and highest-ranked factors were accumulated in the following list:

5. Hayuth, Y. (1985), "Freight Modal–Split Analysis of Air and Sea Transportation", *Logistics and Transportation Review* 21, pp. 389–402.

Principal factors affecting mode choice for freight

Rank order	Factor
1	Total transit time
2	Client deadline
3	Commodity value per ton
4	Stock-related elements
5	Freight rate charges
6	Wharfage charges
7	Commodity–volume–weight ratio
8	Product perishability
9	Size of shipment
10	Reliability

No single factor could be isolated as being the principal one for all cargoes in the mode-choice process. There are different considerations for each and every commodity. Total transit time was quoted most frequently as the most significant variable when evaluating a preferred transport mode. The importance of this factor stems not only from the speed difference between air and sea carriage, but also from such variables as the frequency of service, the length of time needed for clearing goods in seaports or airports, and the distance between the terminal and the market. In a study of mode choice for shipments between Melbourne and Sydney, the delivery-time factor was also very high in the ranking order.[6]

Among the top ten factors involved in the choice process, three are related to the nature of the product. The volume–weight ratio of a commodity plays an important role because of the differences between ocean and air transportation in the common practice of establishing a basis for the freight rate. In general, the relationship between the physical aspects of a commodity and the variables related to transport technology, which forms the essence of the technological positivist approach in the mode-choice process,[7] was found to be of significant importance, particularly for shippers who have selected the ocean transport mode.

6. Gilmour, P. (1976), "Some Policy Implications of Subjective Factors in the Modal Choice for Freight Movements", *Logistics and Transportation Review*, 12, pp. 39–57.
7. Gray, R. (1982), "Behavioural Approaches to Freight Transport Modal Choice", *Transport Reviews* 12, pp. 61–84.

CHAPTER 9

Intermodality in the future

Containerization may now be considered a mature system. Most liner trade routes between industrial countries are entirely containerized, and the level of penetration of containers into the liner trade between the developed and developing countries has surpassed the half-way point. No radical changes either in the design or in the methods of operation of container vessels, cranes, and yard equipment were realized between the 1960s and the early 1980s. Intermodality represents both a new phase of containerization and a significant transport development. Although not an entirely new concept, intermodality has been developing at an accelerated pace since the early 1980s, trying as it were to carve out for itself a meaningful place in the freight transportation system in general and within the shipping industry in particular. The comprehensive point of view and the adoption of the "total concept" perspective for the transport chain; the level of involvement and investments by shipping lines, ports, and railways in intermodal transport; the trend toward rationalization of conventional transport systems and increased cooperation and coordination between transport modes — these phenomena, furthermore, all act to substantiate the claim of a new era in freight transportation.

Unlike containerization, the implementation of which was essentially similar in the United States, Europe, the Far East, and even the developing countries, the practice of intermodality has varied considerably in different parts of the world. It will probably continue to so vary. Containerization was, above all, a technological innovation, one requiring a great deal of standardization in transport units and equipment. Intermodality, by contrast, is characterized by organizational features, which are more exposed to the influences of local and national regulatory policies and political structures.

In the United States, the relaxation in less than a decade of the regulatory environment surrounding the different transport industries (trucks, railways, shipping lines, and airlines) has enhanced the development of intermodality. Deregulation is certainly a prime factor behind the structural changes taking place in the United States transport scene. The level of commitment made by American and foreign shipping lines alike, as well as by North American railways, seaports, and inland container terminals, reveals that the intermodal concept in that part of the world has advanced beyond the trial period. The arguments that are being voiced about the validity and profitability of the concept may have some merit; however, they are primarily short term in their scope and outlook. These negative charges will not change the course of development of intermodality once the opportunities that the concept can offer have been revealed, even on a partial basis.

In continental Europe, the implementation of the intermodal concept takes a different shape, dictated by inherent differences in political structure and transport infrastructure. The continent's fragmented transport industry, its multi-national regulatory policies, and the complexity of institutional frameworks place major constraints on the development of long-haul through-transport movements. The constraints are potentially serious in that the quality and efficiency of a total transport system are measured against the weakest link in the transport chain. Consequently, less than full cooperation by one country or a not wholehearted attempt at coordination by one transport mode may prove the entire system deficient.

Despite the objective difficulties, intermodality has not been ignored in Europe. It just takes a different direction than in the United States. Double-stack trains are not a valid option in most parts of Europe because of the electrification of the railway system; on the other hand, intermodal movements involving barge transportation are at a much more advanced stage than in North America. The interrelation between domestic and international intermodal transport in Europe will be affected by the differences in national rate structures, different preferences in rail cars, and the average distance of transport haul, which differ from those across the Atlantic. In certain aspects of intermodality, European transport organizations attempt to follow in the steps of the North Americans. The efforts of the ports of Rotterdam and Antwerp to improve their rail services to the hinterland is one example. In other aspects, however, they take a leading role. The effort that each of these two ports in particular has invested in upgrading their position in the physical distribution chain has propelled them into the forefront of seaports attempting to integrate themselves into intermodality.

The prospect of the diffusion of intermodality to the developing world is not too positive in the foreseeable future. It is very difficult to perceive a repetition of the huge step that countries in South East Asia, for example, have taken with respect to containerization. It is not only the fact that many of the developing countries are still lagging behind in the development of containerized facilities; the condition of the inland transport networks also throws up a major obstacle. The low level of importance that intermodality receives on the priority list of the developing countries, therefore, is hardly surprising.

With the advance of the intermodal concept, the centre of gravity of transportation activities and developments is gradually shifting from the sea-side to the inland segments of the system. Cargo-handling methods at the port and vessel design have been the focal points of the containerization era. Most of the developments of the intermodal concept, on the other hand, have been taking place on land. Newly designed rail rolling stock, inland intermodal freight stations, and improvement of the port's land-side operations have drawn most of the attention when it comes to the physical aspects of intermodal transportation. Moreover, the relative importance of inland transportation in the total transport chain has been increasing as a direct result of the fact that the lion's share of the costs involved in a door-to-door service on most international trade routes relate to inland transportation modes, not to the ocean voyage. During the containerization period, the needs of the ocean carriers dictated developments, whether in seaports or other elements related to container handling. The standard container sizes of 20 and 40 feet constitute a clear indication of that trend. It is, ironically, the recent changes in the dimensions of container units that provide yet another example of the changing trend in mode importance. The introduction of high-cube, 45 or 48-foot containers signifies the greater weight of inland transport needs and the consideration given to them. Based on the economic rationale of the total transport system, it is reasonable to anticipate a continuation of the trend to longer than 40-foot containers and trailers in the future. Finally, from the shipper's perspective, the selection of a carrier for the international trade movement is now less dependent on a specific shipping service or available shipping line; more depends on the "package" that can be received for the total origin-destination transport journey. Such "packages" will increasingly include space-charter agreements or service contracts offered by "third party" organizations, such as the land-based NVOCCs, or even by total transport companies.

The present is characterized by an overtonnaged shipping industry, a slow rate of international trade growth, and a depressed level of freight rates; in this gloomy situation, intermodal transportation has become a means by which shipping lines can increase their business. In order to survive, shipping companies have to rationalize their services, either by way of horizontal integration through the forming of consortia and joint agreements or by a process of vertical integration. It is not the first time that in a period of change shipping lines have had to pool their resources in order to meet the challenge and subscribe the necessary capital. The well-known consortia formed in Europe in the late 1960s and early 1970s provide an earlier example. Now, in addition, the involvement of shipping companies in other than sea-side operations, and certainly the extent of such involvement, is a direct consequence of the intermodal concept. Various forms of joint service agreements among shipping lines have become quite common in the mid-1980s, and probably will dominate some of the main trade routes in the future. The small or single shipping company, although it will find it difficult to compete on the high seas, will carve its own niche in ocean-borne trade, either in shorter runs or in a feeder-service role whereby they can exploit their flexibility and small-scale operation.

The liner conferences have survived many critical problems in the past. The intermodal concept provides yet another hurdle, but this one might prove more difficult to overcome than ever before. The total transport system is outside the traditional jurisdiction of the conference, let alone being beyond their control. Shipping lines operating on a global or nearly global scale not only traverse the routes of several liner conferences, but may also find it impossible to coordinate their operations within or even with a conference. The interest and responsibility of such lines are considerably wider in space and scope and include inland transport legs, as well. Moreover, the growing trend towards and importance of the multi-modal transport company, which offers a shipper the whole range of services for the through-transport journey, including a through rate, presents a major challenge to the survival of the liner conference system.

The transportation literature and experience are replete with cases of transport competition. With intermodality, the competition has not become less fierce; but the traditional framework and rules of transport competition have been challenged. The stretching of shipping lines and transport companies beyond their traditional range of operations has brought to any given region more transport elements, competing on a wider range of services and trade routes. The growing involvement of shippers' organizations and NVOCCs in the total transport system adds still another dimension to the complexity of the new competitive environment.

The efforts of all parties involved in the physical distribution process are focused on gaining control of the cargo as close to the shipper as possible. Whoever wins such control can channel the consignments along the route that best serves its overall preferences. The future of intermodal transportation, however, will produce not only competition; there will also be greater complementarity among the traditional competitors. The rationale of the intermodal concept calls for more cooperation and for complementary services, based on the assumption that an efficient total transport chain is composed of linked transport modes, each operating on a section of the route, on which it can show a relative advantage. Thus trucking companies may extend their business, not by competing with the railways, but by complementing them. Early signs indicate that complementary services between land and sea or air and sea transport modes open up new opportunities for all modes concerned, and that more such combined services are yet to establish themselves.

Intermodality has recently been faced with a new opportunity. Computerization and communication and information systems have been high on the agenda of every element of the transport industry that foresees its future with intermodality. If containers served as a common denominator for the dawn of intermodality, any advance of the concept is greatly dependent on its ability to provide a direct, on-line computer link and a flow of information between shipper, consignee, customs, and the transport company.

Finally, the future challenge of intermodality can best be met if shipping lines, seaports, and transport companies all adopt a comprehensive, strategic planning approach. A look over the shoulder back just two decades leads to the inevitable conclusion that international freight transportation is an ever-changing system, informed by a great deal of fluctuation in trade demand, supply of vessels, freight rates, technology, and methods of operation. In such an environment, in which decision making is concerned not only with meeting the short-term demands of fluctuating market conditions — this may also be true of many other services — but also with crucial issues related to structural changes, heavy investments, and aborting traditional directions and functions, then the strategic planning approach is a necessity. In the transport industry, which is dynamic in character, let alone in intermodal transportation, which is comprehensive and inclusive in nature, strategic thinking might mean the difference between success and failure.

Strategic planning provides the shipping company with a tool to evaluate its response to short-term changes on one level and to lift this response above myopic considerations in order to evaluate a long-term direction in a flexible, continuous line. It allows identification of key factors involved in any decision-making process and objective determination of the weaknesses of its operation. The latter opportunity is particularly significant to intermodality, for which the weakest link in the chain is the most critical. Strategic planning may help ports to evaluate their role in the changing transport environment and allow port management to take relevant steps toward future directions and investments. A strategic approach, moreover, can navigate the freight transport industry in stormy as well as in calm seas.

Index